POET TOWN
The Poetry of Hastings & Thereabouts

edited by
RICHARD NEWHAM SULLIVAN

with photographs by
MAXINE SILVER

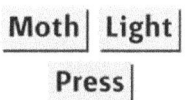

poet town

This book is dedicated to Irina,
with love and gratitude

CONTENTS

CLASSIC POEMS

POET TOWN

The Poetry of Hastings & Thereabouts

Salena Godden

Welcome to the wonderful world of Poet Town.

I will always call Hastings home. I also call poetry home. So writing the introduction for this book feels like I'm showing you around my house, here is the kitchen and here is the hearth. Here is an anchor, a place I know and love and feel safe and held. Here is a book set in my heartland. It is wonderful to be invited to be a part of Poet Town and a great honour to be invited to read these poems first and to be asked to open the door and introduce you to our home.

Poet Town is a book where some truth is shared, some magical inspiration is found and all the weather is weathered. These poems are from here, they are deep and salty, they are lurking in the crash of sea water around the legs of the Pier, as much as they are wafting in the salt and vinegar on your fish and chips. These poems come from a place where the skies are constant and emotional and ever changing, where writing and story telling and gossiping is traditional, is community and is word of mouth. Hastings is a place where poets are born, where poets are found. Hastings is a place where poetry is discovered in long walks along the cliffs, gazing up at the stars and the moon, searching for the horizon. Hastings poetry is rough and raw and real, it is dwelling in the ancient conversations echoing with the haunted click of boot heels in the dead of night. It is poetry the colour of salt water, it is in the smell of seaweed, it is in the froth on your pint. Hastings poetry is precious in the same way you hold on to the hagstone you keep in your pocket as though it were treasure.

I have loved Hastings all of my life. My family and friends are here. I was not born here, but along the coast in Margate. However, my father grew up here. My parents were married here. My paternal grandfather loved living here and was buried here. I have a deep connection to the town. I tell the story in my memoirs:

My Grandpa George bought and lived in the old house on Springfield Road in the 1950s—but way before that his parents lived here, they met in the department store Boots, on Robertson Street in Hastings. In those days, Boots had an art department—his father was an art dealer and picture framer—and his mother worked in the silverware department. They settled in Hastings and ran a small art shop on Norman Road, a ten-minute walk from Springfield Road. The shop hardly made any money and so they also sold cigarettes, tobacco and stationery. They found they still couldn't make ends meet and so they took in lodgers and summer visitors. As a boy Grandpa George remembers losing his bed to guests sometimes and his mother staying up half the night cleaning.

During the Second World War, my Grandpa George was a wireless operator on a tank in the Middle East. He returned to civilian life with medals that he never ever mentioned or displayed. If he ever spoke of the war, it was only to illustrate the importance of manners and kindness. When Grandpa George came home to Hastings he became the verger at Christchurch, St Leonards, and it was during this period he met and married my grandmother, Edith Godden. George became a nurse, and worked at various hospitals including Battle Hospital until he retired.

Christchurch is a beautiful sandstone church in the centre of St Leonards. When I was a kid, on school holidays, I'd often accompany Grandpa George to church to help him change the hymn boards and replace the altar candles. We'd talk in whispers while doing these tasks. I was curious about being permitted up the narrow steps into the bell tower and backstage into the priests' musky dressing rooms, where the cassocks and robes hung like stage costumes. Both my grandparents and then my parents were married in Christchurch. My mother was a go-go dancer and my father a jazz musician. My parents toured with the likes of television game show host Larry Grayson and legendary ska band the Skatalites. Sadly my father isn't here anymore, he died in 1981. I have been told that my father, Paul Godden, was a brilliant musician, that he could play almost anything you put in front of him—the piano, the trumpet, the clarinet, the trombone. He was a drinker and a great laugh down the pub. My mother tells me that as a young man the local police in Hastings knew him by sight and often found him after closing time, singing in the street and along Hastings seafront, and would bring him home to Springfield Road. He hated to wear a suit; when he did it looked like it had been thrown at him and just missed. He was a writer of poetry, a lover of jazz, a wearer of cravats and neckerchiefs. He was a bohemian and a libertine. When I was at the house on Springfield Road I was closest to his life as a boy and young man. The fact that he had lived there, and was a teenager in that very house, was all I had. I knew he was confirmed and that he sang in the choir at Christchurch, and I knew that he read and wrote music and poetry. I imagined he probably composed those songs and poems while walking on Hastings' pebbled beaches, and later as a teenager I often walked along the same beaches and sat under Hastings Pier writing poems and tried to recreate or emulate this.

Hastings is forever the archetypal British seaside holiday resort that needs a holiday, all faded grandeur and peeling façade. So too was our family home on Springfield Road, with the walls still echoing a time when it was full of life, laughter and love. There was a time once when the bricks of that old house vibrated with the laughter and tears of dozens of children who were taken in or fostered here over the years. My grandmother Edith was a member of the Mothers' Union and took in various children who needed care. Soon the house on Springfield Road was filled with temporary foster children, some from London, others local, all allocated to Edith through the church and the union. Edith Godden was killed in a road accident at the top of Springfield Road the year I was born.

I went to the school called The Grove, the lower school was situated right at the bottom of Springfield Road. It was a narrow, crooked and decrepit old schoolhouse, which they have demolished now and rebuilt. Looking back my 1980s school days were deliciously idle: I enjoyed playing along the promenade and on the beaches. Sometimes we'd sneak into the closed-down Lido on the Marina, or go to Alexandra Park to climb trees and play on the swings.

My brother and I liked to go down to the seafront to an amusement arcade called *Out of this World*. For the price of a day pass, you had unlimited plays on all the electronic games, *Pacman* and *Space Invaders*. There was a darkened room that was an all-day music video disco. We were barefoot all summer. We lived on the beach and scooped rivers and irrigated moats around pebbled turrets of wet mud sandcastles. We jumped from rock to rock with nets, paddling in shallow crab pools. Teenage girls in jelly shoes slathered coconut and olive oil on each other's shoulders, cooking themselves in the midday sun, trying hard to get the attention of young wannabe surfers with no real waves to catch who lay on their bellies on their surfboards, basking on a flat green sea. From the beach you could always see the distant lush green of the

West and East Hills, rising like two plump mounds. Walking towards Fairlight, you'd find beautiful places to think or fly a kite. We'd go meandering along the wild, yellow gorse-lined paths of the Fire hills in a daydream.

Hastings Castle was a broken tooth above the chalky, jagged jaws of the cliff face, which in later years became the place for the sweetest flush of first love: teenage secrets, stolen cigarettes, French kisses and bottles of cider. When the tide was out, standing on the rocks and looking back towards land, as far as the eye could see the beaches stretched in shades of mineral, copper and granite, swirls of slate and smooth amber-coloured stones, pieces designed especially for skimming and skipping stones across the water's surface. If you found yourself a lucky pebble with a hole in the middle, they said, you would always return to Hastings. I always thought that was a good thing.

—Extracts from *Springfield Road*

Poet Town is an electric and eclectic celebration of the wealth, health and richness of Hastings heart and soul, of our stories, poetry, mythology, delivered to you from writers and dreamers from all walks of life. To gather everyone together like this is to gather family, is to gather the speakers and the thinkers and doers and the creators in one book, I think it is truly fantastic and joyful and with thanks to the editor and community involved in its creation, I also think this is well overdue.

SALENA GODDEN / HASTINGS 2025

'Beautifully Unharnessed Poets'
A short film presenting some of the best spoken word poets of Hastings

Featuring:

Tara Valentine · Lucas the Peaceful Poet
Thomas BW Barron · Grace Pilkington · Yellow & Green
Katie Taylor · Chris Widda-Beats

Watch here:

tinyurl.com/unharnessedpoets

Directed & Produced by Lauren Estelle Jones
Camera: Daniel Nikolaison | Sound: Alex Collishaw
Filmed at the Rock & Roll Public Library

MODERN POETS

AK Benedict on the West Hill

A Song to Hastings

With its pebbles and its sinking beach,
A sea that 'tempts to maybe reach
The pretty painted houses high,
As white sky-bound the seabirds circle
The people hugged around the shore.
This is Hastings seaside town
Cheery, coastal Hastings.

With cat creeps and twittens sly
As that word from older times.
This is Hastings with steep inclines
And tiny windy alley sneaks, says a no
To me in my wheelchair mode.
This is Hastings seaside town,
A teasing, haunted Hastings.

The sea gulls mewl and poo-poo-poo,
Grabbing ice creams, bags of chips.
Birds bomb Hastings, nips on wings
Loving thermals by the sea.
Guerrilla bird, you're bold to me.
This is Hastings seaside town,
Bright, bawdy, boozy Hastings.

Bumpy path on Rock-a-Nore
To take me near the swelling sea,
An outpost of the windswept cliffs,
Of jagged sand hued geology.
Birds lift on air, as dark waves flare
Against the pebbles constant hiss,
Rattle-shells twist in the brine.
This is Hastings seaside town.
My heart is yours, old Hastings.

Lost in Spaces

Bleary excitement on the children's ward;
I'm almost nine and counting up the stars,
Sharp-bright, distant and unexplored—
Are there rings round Saturn, and red dust on Mars?

On telly the stay-up treat is men in space.
I gaze at the flicker, misty black and white.
The NASA men speak in a hiss, a haste.
We're up from the bed; I'm going to take flight.

I want to float off into weightless skies;
This is Major Pen to Ground Control.
Look back at Planet Earth through different eyes,
Be mistress of the moon that I patrol.

But broken kids don't star in big space shows.
You never see us scorch across your screen.
We do not compute—as every robot knows.
Danger, Will Robinson! Life is not a TV scene.

Yet I yearn for the great beyond;
Commencing countdown, engines—go.
To boldly reach where no cripple girl has gone!
Horizon's wide, I won't look back below.

I'm rolling through the once-sealed door
And floating in a most unexpected way.
Planet Pen evolves, a universe to explore,
And yes. There's everything to say.

A Spoken Word Love Poem

Candlelight and stars
making patterns
quiver on the sea
in a restaurant
by Hastings Pier.

I toy with my mackerel,
full of thoughts
of when it swam
in its
happy swimmy sea.

My lover's blue eyes catch mine,
misty hazel from Merlot.
He lifts my hand
across the frosty linen tablecloth
and says, I wrote you a poem.

I blush
above my fish floating on the briny white plate

Tell me now, I sigh,
what poetry lurks
in that head
behind those glinting eyes,
what words will come
from the upturn
of your sweet mouth?

I still my breath.
The stars pause in their
tiny brilliance.

The world waits.

Tits! he says
I love your tits!
Your bestest bits

Is your tits.
Fit tits, pert tits.
Tits to rate.
Your tits are fucking great!

I spear the cold mackerel
through its belly,
heart chilled and shaking,
and wonder at the world.

A Sonnet for Blues and Rain

I heard the blues seduce the rain tonight
While owls sang songs to say that spring won't come.
They lurk in trees and whisper far from sight.
The blank sky shrugs down darkness. There among
The leaves I hid my heart and head and tears,
Drenched in the song the Blues Man gave to me,
Longing in my blood made sweeter with years.
Dark branches sway, they're full of melodies.
It's not love lost that aches inside my soul—
It's his true words that cry across the rain.
He sings the howling blues, he's in control,
Heals all my scars tonight, laps up my pain.
I will live for hidden owls, trees and hope,
The Blues Man's electric kaleidoscope.

Tell Good People Good Things

Tell each other you love each other.
Say love. Show your love. Speak it.

Do not wait to talk to a flower
in the hope the dead will hear the love
you could've said before.

Do not wait to talk to headstones
and weep at faded photographs.

Please do not die with all unsaid
and then haunt your loved ones
appearing in night and shadow and dream.

You are alive now. So love now.

Tell your good people all the good things.
Tell each other you love each other.

Do not wait to softly weep to flickering candles
or cry about your love to a flower too late.

Say love. Show your love. Share it.

Under The Pier

Under the pier
I'd meet you here
on Saturday lunchtimes
in technicolours and rainbows.

There were four of us that day
walking along Bottle Alley
I'd touch shards of saffron-coloured glass
pressed into the bleached concrete
and wonder what came in yellow bottles.

Ceri balanced along the ledge
like a gymnast on a beam
her wild gold hair trapped
in the corners of her mouth.

Claire wore thick mascara
in turquoise and royal blue
her eyelashes were insects
bluebottles and beetles legs.

Becky was tall and gangly
we talked about suicide.
We believed 1987
was gonna be just like 1967
as we swigged from the Thunderbirds red
fifty pence more expensive
than the blue
but we were all sick of Scrumpy.

The four of us sheltered there from
the rain and the boys and our parents.
It was our secret place
that nook and ledge

with our backs against the sea wall
our voices drowned out
by the crashing of waves

a wash of froth and brine
an echo of footsteps
across the soft rotting wood
of the boardwalk above us.
There were gaps between the planks
prisms of watery light
brown broken pipes emptied
in slurps of sewage.

Lightening flashed
between the rusty barnacled legs
of the dear old lady pier
and the magic mushrooms
made the sea all blood and ink.

We shared ten B&H
bubble-gum lip gloss
smeared and slipped off the tip
and the lip of the bottle
and we sang 'Purple Rain'
memorised the words like a prayer.

With a tiny crumb of hash
we huddled around the light
we cupped our hands
to make the spliff, right,
we were grounded
because we had love bites
we were nearly fifteen
and we had catfights.

We swore to be best friends forever
that our children would play together
one for all and all for one
forever and ever ...

And as the storm died
the rain stopped and
God was a solitary shaft of sunlight
hitting the sea with a silver path to the horizon,

Under the pier
I'll meet you
here.

While Justice Waits

there they go again
filling your mouth
with their name

there they go again
adding more weight
to your burden
there they go again
giving you all the anxiety
whilst telling you not to panic
when the panic is rooted in
centuries of ...
there they go again
there they go again

there they go again
contradicting their own rules
double speak and double standards

there they go again
your dead are statistics
your ghosts live in hashtags

there they go again
getting away with murder
but calling it anything else

there they go again
doing nothing
as your vulnerable
and sick and dying
need all your love and care
and your living need all of your
focus, energy and time
there they go again
filling your plate
with their jobs
and the work

they should do
as your elected leaders
there they go again,
dominating your thoughts
so no work can get done
there they go again
grimacing on the front page
hogging the limelight
with this theatre of
performative cruelty

there they go again
suffocating light and hope
like a pillow held fast over the face
of the kicking and struggling truth

there they go again
consuming all the oxygen
and rewriting history

there they go again
like it's all about them
but it is because of them
and it is in spite of them

there they go again
obscuring the facts
blurring the edges
blinkering the horse
filtering the picture

there they go again
there they go again
there they go again
and it is not the names of the dead
nor the name of the nurse
nor the name of the innocent
but their name in your mouth

how can it be?
that when you wake in the night
wailing and mourning and hurting
they are marching on your tongue
they are renting your insomnia

there they go again
using your anguish as garnish
using your defence as an attack
using your fear to divide you
using your rage to pass draconian laws
using your pain to sell shit back to you
using your grief to decorate newspapers
using your anger to kill you
because there they go again
there they go again
there they go again
casting an ass in the lead role
the wealthy politicians in the spotlight
the hideous clown gets top billing
the monster as the headline act
your horror gets a walk on part
your mourning cries are extras
your fury is the chorus line
your humanity the supporting cast

while justice waits in the wings

When They Took Her Away

When they took her away
she wasn't kicking or screaming.
It was as though
she saw it coming
like she'd been buying time.
I wanted her to shake her fist
tell us she'd show us one day
I thought she'd put up a fight
instead,

when they took her away—
they didn't take her away exactly,
but they led her away—
I saw her lips in a silent whistle
she was exhaling with one breath
she was blowing out a candle
at the end of the night.

As she got into the back seat
they protected her head
she stared, waited patiently
as they secured her seat belt.
She didn't turn
to look at us
staring out the window
but I like to think
I saw the faintest smile
playing in the corner of her mouth
as the car pulled away.

She'll get plenty of bed rest
where she's going
books and telly
free hot meals.
It's probably what she needs.
Come to think of it

it's probably what we all need.

ED BOXALL

The Gods of Green Summer are Awake

On this day the streets belong to The Gods of Green Summer.

Today is their proud procession.
They have come alive for this fast-flickering season.
They call us mortals from cafés, cars and carpeted rooms
to the wild adventure of Summer.

Now I am ready for ivy night rambles
I am ready for all-night raggle tangles and thornyscratch
   scrambles.

I am ready for Summer to begin.

To the Gods of Green Summer

Gods of Green Summer I solemnly swear
to drink green sunshine with scarecrows
Gods of Green Summer I solemnly swear
to burn my list of things to do and bury my phone
Gods of Green Summer I solemnly swear
to eat cold custard from a broken mug in a rhododendron bush
Gods of Green Summer I solemnly swear
to leap from the witch's cauldron remade and reborn.
Gods of Green Summer I solemnly swear
to run along the harbour arm, dive into the sea,
and surface with a fish in my teeth.
Now I am ready for Summer.
And I see so clearly
how long, and wide, and deep it can be.

No Trains Home

The Gods of Green Summer
breathed a deep blanket of ivy over the railway station.
They tied roots around the train wheels,
sewed nettle thickets through the tracks,
and conjured rosy hot mesmeric air,
so the station staff
talk visionary gibberish
or sleep in the branches of the bright trees
that now burst through Platform 4.

There will be no trains home.
This trip to the seaside
will last forever.

BRIAN MOSES

Those 1066, Battle of Hastings, Re-enactment Blues

I drew the short straw
for the role I would play,
which meant that I spent
the best part of the day
lying flat on my back
stretched out in the mud,
too close to a cowpat
and streaked with fake blood.

And I've got a feeling we're going to lose.
It's those 1066, Battle of Hastings, re-enactment blues.

It's like supporting Tottenham
and knowing you always lose
to Man. U. at Old Trafford
and then suddenly there's news
that totally unexpectedly
the score's 3-2 to you,
and you think if that can happen
maybe this can happen too.

But I've got a feeling we're going to lose,
it's those 1066, Battle of Hastings, re-enactment blues.

And I'm hoping that maybe today
us Brits could even win,
that the arrow could miss Harold's eye
and the French army swiftly give in.
If only for a day we could
reverse the course of history,
send the French off home
and celebrate a British victory.

But I've got a feeling we're going to lose,
it's those 1066, Battle of Hastings, re-enactment blues.

And really I know it won't happen,
the fatal arrow will still fly by
with Harold's name written on it,
heading straight for his eye.
And that will be the signal
for British soldiers to retreat,
a hoof print on my thigh
as I contemplate defeat.

And I know for sure that we're going to lose,
(and I wish I'd worn more sensible shoes)
it's those 1066, Battle of Hastings, re-enactment blues.

Dragon Path

for Crowhurst Village School, who gave this name to a path
in their playground

Nothing will be the same as before
once you've drawn a dragon to your door,
once a dragon knows where to find you
you'll always have to look behind you,
always have to take great care
once you summon a dragon from its lair.
And it won't be any kind of joke
if you see flames, if you smell smoke
or wake to find in dread of night,
half the village set alight.
Then next day finding your head teacher
protecting the school from this fearful creature,
flameproofing the roof, soundproofing the doors
to block out the noise of its dragony roars.
While you're inside, preparing for SATS,
the dragon is feasting on barbecued cats.
Avoiding the dragon will drive you insane.
I suggest you rename your path 'Sweet Hamster Lane.'

Dungeness

At first sight, the landscape
looks a mess,
like a giant's child dropping
his building bricks
and then kicking them around for a bit
to see where they settle.
People go there looking for
a different sort of somewhere,
it's that jumble sale kind of place
where you might just find anything.
The birds go more for order there,
neatly spaced seagulls on telephone wires,
pairs of pigeons on chimney pots.
Aside from the power station's paraphernalia
and two tubular light towers,
everything else crouches low,
grits its teeth, turns its back
on the winds that whip up the Channel.
A small train huff-puffs its way
along a single track;
It's either an ending or a beginning
depending on how you look at it.
It's a place without make-up,
no frills or fashions,
doesn't care if it's late,
can't be bothered to dress for dinner.
It's a take it or leave it
sort of place, no fuss.
But nevertheless, I like Dungeness.
I like the way it shrugs its shoulders,
couldn't care less.

A K BENEDICT

The Selection Process

First thing I notice—the interviewer's a clown.
Pancaked-face, patchwork coat,
curls the colour of Post-It notes,
'Do sit down,' he says, thrusting
out a white-gloved hand.
The buzzer sends shocks to my armpit.

This must be the wrong room.
It's jostling with balloon dogs,
'Happy Birthday!' stretched over their bellies.
'Is this the interview for Financial Controller?' I ask.
The clown flicks and frowns
through my CV: 'I see you left your last job

after only one year. What's to stop
you doing the same thing here?
Tell me—what's your greatest flaw?
And what would you do if you saw
your mother stealing the Mona Lisa?'
I open my mouth to reply,
he smothers it with custard pie.

The team building begins.
Other applicants enter. Dressed
to the nine-to-fives, shoes shined, noses blown,
we're whittled down to statues and chairs.
Against a soundtrack of balloon dogs popping,
we run in ragged ellipses.

During sleeping lions,
the clown crouches, inches from my face,
and whispers, 'You can't win'.
He checks his paint in a mirror.
His grin smells of whiskey
and fish sticks.

I'm in the last three. In the waiting room
we drink jelly-sweet tea, eat chips
from spreadsheet cones. 'We'll let you know,'
the clown says, winking, handing us a goody bag each.
Inside mine is a compact and face-paint
stale cake wrapped up in a contract.

REANNA VALENTINE

I'm Going Over The Country Park

Only on sweltering July afternoons
Are the crickets' hums
In perfect harmony with ozone molecules

Time unspools
Like ferns did in June
Boot laces tied too loosely

I have ancestors
Who are not quite yet ancestors
Who can't go hiking any more
Who I should travel to visit soon
And ones that show up without warning
In the Grand Hotel, Eastbourne

Living and lifeless limbs my friend hid in
When they were facing everything
Bare branch tips
Armpits sprouting mosses and lichen
Upside-down years hanging onto centuries
You old oak survivor

Recent ancestors aid in my night-time workings out
And I wish, again, that they would show up in the day
Without warning

All the small flowers are blooming

The steps to the nudist beach
Keep being stolen by landslides
Clay soil and sandstone are reliably unreliable

Those ancestors four generations prior, or more
Seem unreachable
I harbour vague intentions to learn ritual

My phone clock is a dancing forest sprite
Full of tricks blown in
On the southern wind
Time is uncertain
I wouldn't have thought to look at all
Had my pen not broken

My ancestors are intermingled
In the waves
In the twigs
They weren't from here
But they are here
I will walk until I find them

The Big Sainsbury's

It's Spring, and Kerry arrives for her shift
at the big Sainsbury's.

8-4.

She'd rather have worked 10-6
but nothing is ever easy and life
is very difficult.
One month ago, a film crew had been in to
make a reality TV programme
about

Britain's Unsung Heroes.

That's what they kept saying as they pressed
the camera hard into her cheeks.

They said, "You are one of Britain's unsung heroes."

"Oh right," said Kerry.

"What are you doing now?"
they said with their
tongues lolling
out of their
mouths

and their equipment scattered over the aisle
like a nasty assault
course.
"I'm stacking the alternative milks," said Kerry.

"And how did your mother die?"

"Oh," said Kerry.
Oh.
Oh.
Oh.

"She was hit by the number 91 bus to Wadhurst," said Kerry.

"What's that now?" the producer said
with his hands stuffed down
his jeans.

"Could you say that again, but facing the camera?"

Kerry turned and the terrible fat lens
of the camera pushed close.

She dropped the alternative milk
and rushed back down
the aisle.

She stayed in the staff room
for the rest of the day.

Now it's Spring.

The show was on TV last night,
but it wasn't called

Britain's Unsung Heroes

it was called

Britain's Filthiest Supermarket.

For some reason they'd included the footage of Kerry
dropping the
milk.

Her face looked raw and cold and horrible on the TV screen.

But nothing is ever easy, and life is very difficult,
so, Kerry pushes through the gang of elderly
ladies taking pictures of her
with their flip phones
and walks through
the shop door
with her
head

high.

The Dead

In the pink light of Dom's Doughnuts,
Linda sees the ghost of
her first husband

the bastard

who died in 1997 after a blow to
the head during a game of pool
one Thursday evening

at

The Lord Nelson.

They never caught the boy who did it.

He's looking out towards the sea,
holding a polystyrene
cup of coffee.

One hand on his fat stomach.

The police had come to the house
to deliver the news but Linda was
out at rehearsals for

The King and I.

She tries to take a photo of him on
her phone but she hasn't quite
worked out the camera yet so
all she gets is the sleeve
of her new
cardigan.

She can't think of anyone she'd have
shown it to
anyway.

He's wearing the shoes she bought him from
Marks, and a jacket she doesn't recognise.

She begins to feel faintly

irritated.

He's not waiting for her.

He's not waiting for anyone.

He's just standing there
with his hand on
his stomach,

long dead,

in the pink light of Dom's Doughnuts.

She turns abruptly to cross the
road and fails to see
the wing mirror
of the number
20 bus
which clips her

hard

and knocks her glasses off her face.

In the clamour afterwards,
as people rush to help,
she hears someone
whistling,

"Hello Young Lovers."

The bastard.

ARMAND GARNET RUFFO

Buffalo Bill's Wild West Show Comes
to Hastings

Indians of the type familiarised by the illustrations
which grace the covers of penny 'blood and thunder'
publications, Mexican cowboys, handy-men and cavalry
of many nations, herded together in orderly confusion,
if such a term is permissible, and the demonstrations
they gave of feats of horsemanship, sharp-shooting,
lassoing, and other accomplishments born of long practice
in far parts of the world were indeed a revelation.

—Hastings Observer, August 22, 1903

Archie made sure he was first in line.
  He had arranged to go with his friend McCormick.
    But all day he could hardly keep himself still.
      Five hours to show time he was itching to go.
      Finally he couldn't stand it any longer.
      He would go ahead and hold seats.
          When McCormick arrived he spotted Archie
          talking to one of the Red Indians.

To see them chatting one would have thought they were mates,
or better yet, brothers. Blood brothers! You know
like in the westerns.

Wa-Sha-Quon-Asin
He Who Walks By Night

Because you must
  There's no one else
  You're the first
    The vanguard
You're the trail itself

Night is forever
It's a feeling
  vast as Lake Biscotasing
    high as a white pine
It's a moon that cares for you
Stars that escort you
Beasts that watch
  It's the edge
the private

At night the wind feigns sleep
  You hear the slightest stirring
    Everything is something else
Everything is free
Anything can happen

Morning After, Toronto, 1936

After the kisses
and handshakes,
the party's over
and the past goes home
with the visitors.

At least you expect it to.

What's it like to sit up all night
with wives
dead
or as good as dead,
each one taking her turn?

To emerge from your den
(of books? of leaves?)
pierced yellow eyes
stabbed by daylight,
eyes caught
oozing memory.

What's it like?
It's like fire
or firewater, in your mouth
while you are trying to explain.
It's like death— that's it
to talk to the dead.

Grey Owl, 1937

Hastings must be included. I don't care what city
has to be cut from the itinerary, but Hastings
is the one place I want on the tour.
I get a puzzled look. I know we're booked solid as ice,
sold out, tied up, and running on empty,
but I'm adamant. I've got friends there,
who helped me convalesce during the war,
who took care of me,
were kind to me. And we of the old school
never forget our friends. Sure enough,
my publisher, the head honcho of this whirlwind extravaganza,
finds a free afternoon
and squeezes in my request.

December 14, driving out from London, I am on my way back
to the land of what I thought was no return,
and I find myself eager as one of my... (no I won't say it)
even though I know someone in the audience
might easily pick me off, accuse me
of being nothing more than an old school mate.
Archie is that you? I can hear them now.
Yet, there's no need for alarm. Did I not paddle effortlessly
through this same route a couple of years ago
on my last tour without running aground?
Did they not rush up to me for my autograph
like everywhere else? So why should this time
be any different?

And even if there were a problem brewing,
I would risk it all for a chance to see Aunt Ada
and Carrie's reaction
when I tell them that a week ago their Archie
gave a Command Performance at Buckingham Palace,
and not only saw the Royal Family
but actually spoke to them and shook the hand
of the King, himself. Called him brother.
What do you think of that!

I'll say. Can't go any higher.
And I know they will be pleased pink, if not astounded
and speechless, to know
that I haven't merely made something of myself,
but have risen far beyond what anyone thought
of me, beyond their piddling imaginations
to the very height of kings.

Tim Rich on the Beacon Track

Osiris is slain and his remains distributed about the Internet

I am being scattered as information
across the desert nightlands
of our transactional universe

In the sands and in the reeds
are lost shards of me: data seeds
cast by the side of the path

There is so much of us we let go:
things I'd forgotten about myself
and there are parts of you here too

yet calling out brings nothing
but a mute ba, cold mouthfuls
of unspeakable dust

and now come the harvesters
extracting the crop, so to sell us back
a replica of our wholeness: all

these corporate gods pretending
to be Isis, when they're really
the children of Set

Forever impossible

All of us down here in the dark
and you lying there on your back
in a deep bath of sunlight, toe
pointed towards grinning Saturn
as our muttered devotions rise
to be ignored, of course
your senses attuned only
to the faceless strangers
of everywhere else

It's true I want a piece of you
but not some cold wart of rock
from a sea of tranquility, more
a shimmer of the inner you
impressed on the sensitivities
of my recently upgraded device
so I can recast your essence
through the filter of me, framed
as an expression of my self

Yet, you are forever impossible
to hold, always exiting stage right
in a blur of laughter, leaving
my literal technology stammering
in the presence of your unsayable glow
and now with each failed capture
I want even more
for you to stay
uncaught

On the difficulty of selecting
the right frame for a portrait

At times
you remind me
of an owl
lost at sea
listening for what
has already gone
from our world

But perhaps
choosing a salt path
over waves
is how you
sharpen
the taste
of your prey

Deer

The skin on our wrist
is so tender, untroubled
by those arterial lines
at work below

Friend remarked (because
I hadn't realised) *sometimes*
in moments of concern
you pinch your pulse

I know a woman with lyrics
inked down her arm
to where a knit of scar
holds her hand

I said to her once *our skin*
just there, it's like vellum
and the word fell as a deer
pierced. She laughed, *yes*

the skin on our wrist is
so tender, as a balloon before
it's blown into shape
and after

ALICE DENNY

Caroline

These days she thinks, she's like Caroline
Pretty in pink, in the song
So happy, sixteen and now one of the girls
Though she carries her own flowers home
But, at least she knows—and as the song goes
she feels oh so pretty in pink

She sings and is skipping to radio tunes
Smiles as strange faces pass by
Not caring what anyone chooses to think
Nor daring to let herself cry
For at last she knows and as the song goes
She looks oh so pretty in pink

The dark days behind her, she's off to the park
Perhaps to have fun with new friends
Why should she feel anxious, it's long before dark?
And that is where her story ends
But, hey, it just goes to show how prejudice grows
When they know you're so pretty in pink.

And the world should know
As now heaven knows
she was
oh
so
pretty
in
pink.

JUSTIN COE

ALL THIS POET HAS IS HER TRUTH!

and her wit and the weight of her wisdom
and a feel for the cool river's rhythm
and some glasses to sharpen her vision
and a cat in her lap who will listen

ALL THIS POET HAS IS HER TRUTH!

and perhaps paper scraps she can write on
and a room late at night with the light on
and some out of date biscuits to bite on
and the will of a quill that will fight on

ALL THIS POET HAS IS HER TRUTH!

and an eye for the faraway planets
and a regard of the moon and its habits
and a hat that is overdramatic
and some water to help with the tablets

ALL THIS POET HAS IS HER TRUTH!

and even if she struggles to spell it
she has a nose that knows how to smell it
and a tongue and some teeth that can tell it
and a book. And a bookshop to sell it

ALL THIS POET HAS IS HER TRUTH!

and an ear to hear insects and giants
and a love and a loathing of silence
and the courage to take on the tyrants
and some lies that need careful appliance

but apart from all that...

ALL THIS POET HAS IS HER TRUTH!
And her TRUTH is what gives her her license

The Poetry Hotel

Pack up your troubles
And pull on your boots
Take your strengths and your struggles
Fill your pockets with truths
Stop stressing. Start dreaming
Bid your family farewell
Tell them you're leaving for an evening
At The Poetry Hotel

Where there's a room of adventure
Behind every door
And you can be at the centre
Of this world you explore
You've a thirst to be quenched
You've a hunger to quell
And your dreams only make sense
At The Poetry Hotel

It takes in the broken
It takes in the bruised
Its arms are flung open
To the lonely and confused
Come here to be free
Or to relax or rebel
Be who you must be
At The Poetry Hotel

You don't need any pennies
Just a pen is OK
Tune out from the telly
Find the words you must say
You can make your own heaven
You can create your own hell
It's all at your discretion
At The Poetry Hotel

And when you've written your fears out
And your story's been told
And you've cried all your tears out
But your dinner's gone cold
You'll come home 'cos you must do
But still under the spell
Of the room you have to go back to
in The Poetry Hotel

Bridges

We were walking over Blackfriars Bridge together,
when my dad said,
"I wonder who built this bridge?
Whose hands drew up the plans?
Who decided what it should be made of?
Who knew what height and length it had to be
to have the strength to hold its weight?
When you get older you think like this," he said.
"You wonder what you've done in your life
and what you'll leave behind.
I'm not sure what I will leave behind—
but you might, Justin,
with your talent,
you might leave something.
Something.
Though it won't be any money."

BRIAN DOCHERTY

Edward Lear in The Horse & Groom

Well, I was out on Primrose Hill one day
and I observed a daytime fireball, that's
the rarest type of meteor, and I said
to my friend, 'I wish it would land on
Parliament, that would wake them up,
perhaps they would start talking sense';
my friend just stared at me and replied
'Oh Mr Lear, are you some kind of Radical?'
'Not at all, I just desire a better life.'
'Go to Hastings, it's the new Brighton.'

So I did, I've been coming here ever since,
first the Old Town, then Burton St. Leonards,
such a superior class of person over here,
some of whom even say they like my work.
Now that's a sure sign of quality, and if
I am invited to a party, I'll sing for my
supper; during the day I write or draw,
I walk to Rock-a-Nore, and take my
sketchbook, the fishermen are used to
me now, don't bother asking what I do.

Today the daffodils are blowing their
trumpets, this morning I woke with this
line in my head, 'the owl and pussycat
must have friends'; *Who are they* I thought.
I looked out of my window on the Marina,
chanted 'The owl and pussycat went to sea'
and they took me with them before breakfast,
it's amazing how far nonsense will take you;
I'm not Wordsworth, could be Byron for a day,
except he wouldn't like our shingly shore.

FIONA PITT-KETHLEY

Goat Show at the Town and Country Fair

The show was due to start at two o'clock;
one judge, white-coated, entered up some names;
a tousled Toggenburg and herd looked on.
The owner, rumpled as his goat, had two
grey upright feathers in his hat, like horns.
Some half hour late, the others came along:
large spotted Anglo-Nubians, Saanens,
blow-dried white kids, another Toggenburg.
The first, bored to malevolence, shat round.
Her class was next (a second out of two).
Her bloke, disconsolate, questioned the judge
and went off scratching his short beard. The rest
stood round in groups or knelt on half-bald knees
stained by the grass. The Anglo-Nubians
posed like a nest of tables by the ropes.
I sat down on the only patch of turf
left currant-free. A chocolate kid crept up,
fresh from undoing someone's Indian skirt,
and kissed me just like Andrew Marvell's nymph's
young fawn, a pleasant moment till I saw
it press its tender lips against the bold
triangularly-folded rectums of
its peers. "She's been so good," her mistress said.
"It's her first show." Eight classes on, after
some small resentments, almost every goat
has a rosette, red, blue, or green. Four wait
for "Best in Show", ("Reserve Best", too,
a category that's seldom found in life).
"This year", one owner whispers gratefully,
"they didn't pick up his receding chin."

IAIN SINCLAIR

from Marine Court Rendezvous

At night, standing on the balcony, as on the stern of a mock-up of the *Titanic*, you catch glimpses of blue, the trapped lightning of television sets playing in empty rooms, in rooms through which strangers pass, meet, touch, pour drinks, iron their clothes, slump and smoke. The constant argument between the actual (random documentation of the senses) and computer-generated visions and fictions (old movies on the loop, dead divas in their hot prime) is out there, painting the town or reflected in spectral colours on the grey fact of the English Channel. Lost souls ponder the philosophical conundrum: are they viewing *Rear Window* or are they themselves unrehearsed actors performing for other witnesses lurking in the darkness? When does a building decide that its only future is as a posthumous set?

Ordinary Rendition

there were two doctors to visit
in outlying places near a stinking river
one with his face sliding loose or locked
stiff as a till drawer, the other
a hot rivet cooling in his brain
the world's a crock of shit, Stalingrad
he said, gazing from the suburban window
there's a lot of it out there
daylight leaking, eyes onion-white
the fools want absolution, curs
chew on poisoned meat, house set back
from the road, a Sephardic Jew and a junkie
fighting over capitals, scorched earth
prescriptions to fill, whelps to deliver
and worth it, keeping women out of the equation
'most of them want to take their clothes off'
            you can use a line
ugly as the Millennium Dome, trapped in east coast
America ministering to the dead: witnesses agents
it doesn't mean the same thing when
they tell you it's going to be shot in Denmark

I don't want to be god, he said, I'm not qualified

Moleman Tunneller Found Dead

'His name was Blair and he liked to eat shaving soap.'

the moment of standing behind the window
above the sea, listening to an old poet
a dead poet declaim his alpine
sermons and in the drift of difference
    the wave repeats, his mind
was margarine, it seems more open than it
actually was or had ever been,
in lack of grip and true affection,
the ocean reflected in the curtain of
words, lost and returned through
acts of vegetal generosity, perfect pitch
knowing the world is so much better than
    it is: fecund, gracious and fond

Marine News East

* budget wines & football papers
* sky screen café bar
* blue-can lager & cut-price spirits
* lesbian knitting tea room
* kurdish maximart
* rust-boarded unit
* art forums I & II
* alzheimer's society
* armenian bar
* ice-cream parlour
* ex-catalogue furniture dump
* art house all-day breakfasts
* property rental (sorry no DSS)
* a list of cultural uniqueness in 2 columns
* award winning curry house
 (patronised by Ld. Longford & the Warner Bros)
* vanessa fowler works

and one fat chip mayonnaise-fixed
to the lip of the red letter box

EMMA JOLIFFE

Invisible Girls

If anyone had been watching
they'd have seen your legs were bright white
as you made your way down the boarded-up parade
they'd have seen your knees were knobbly in
Primark hotpants.
And if they'd been looking they'd have noticed
you'd a plaster on your right knee
where you'd skinned it at school
when you rushed to get away from
a teacher on patrol,
that last week of term, all hot and chaotic,
and now it's weeks of holidays
stretching out before you like spilt drinks,
tall shadows,
you call into the takeaway,
confidently order chips.
They take you to the back room,
lured by lurid alcopops, all sticky and fizzy,
you giggle and pass it along,
take a cigarette
and hold it like a pro
but if anyone was looking
they'd see you falter,
for a second, see your smile fall,
they'd see your make up was applied with your finger
they'd see the faded felt-tip on your arm
they'd see your left thumb was puckered from sucking
they'd see your bramble scratches
under the bravado.
We only see you too late
as broken down write-offs,
slag heap scrap heap hard-faced
pieces-smashed poor cows
and we missed
our chance.

Fleur du Mal

If you'll be my *Fleur du Mal*,
I'll be your Baudelaire,
compose you verses in the bath
and stroke your salty hair.

We'll luxuriate in thoughts of death
just like Baudelaire,
Bohemians in reverie
who love to love despair.

I'm your empty skeleton
and you're my cutie mouse
you run around my bones and squeak
within my bodyhouse.

Outside the tempest storms and blows
while we laugh at the rain
together in the twilight dim
too happy in our pain.

Mon coeur, mon coeur, light your own lamp
and shine it round yon room,
lead me to the bitter end
where all our flowers bloom

Multi-horse

I rode the black cable into the wall,
curling with every twist of the wire.
By the time I reached the socket I was atoms,
tiny fire pins, multiple captains of paper,
and that paper was on fire.
I was charged multi-horse and alive
as everything that you see in the spring
when we go walking beside father's old hut
where you kissed me and said,
this was your idea of forever.
How much delight I took in struggling free,
and I now look at me, broken-electric,
disappeared into pure energy.

Flight

Run away chair
run away as fast as you can
on your little sharp legs
get yourself away
put a spring in your step
and shoot down the road
one stiff stick after another,
yes, get gone before he catches you,
puts you in his van
and drives off with your trembling body
to another house.

Can't Stand It

Please keep your distance
If you come closer I'm not responsible.
It's not my fault the ground can't stand it
and the sky begins to break into bits,
the trees go shredding upstream
and the clouds spiral back in scuds.
Look. Honestly. Not me.
The whole grey world is crumbling into ash.
While I'm down here, doing nothing at all.

Is it Okay to take Antidepressants with Gin?

They spoke about medications—
they were both on the same drug
one had been on it
for six months
one for eight years
They spoke about therapy
and discussed
whether or not it worked
one had tried it
one never had

I was glad
that they were talking
so openly about
their mental health

They spoke about exercises
to help combat anxiety—
to write down your worries
so that you can look back
to determine whether or not
they were valid or irrational

I told them I do the same thing
I just call it poetry.

JOHN HENDRICKSE

A Detonated Dream

Touching my jeans to attract attention,
looking at the leather coat, checking out the car.
"Mr. I looks after jour car for you?"

A skinny, ragged black boy,
living in the trash can of an affluent world

Surveying me as his meal ticket,
a man who came to spy on what he left behind, how can
I deny him his request.

"Please Mr take me to the U S of A
with Burgers, space machines and Disneyland"

Affluence personified in an American dream.
Hey boy haven't you heard dey did press a button
en it all did blow up wid one big bang.

A look of apprehension,
"you is not joking wid me, Mister?"

I shook my head,
No. Cross my heart is true.

"Den, Mister you must build it again,
but dis time it mustn't be de same;
dis time you must build it for every single one.

  So dat no little boy
  will
  cry in the wastelands
  will
  die in de wastelands

without his dream ever coming true."

Abstracted from a Plane

Watching from this great height
I see brown-grained terrafirma
drawn in different colours against the earth

Fragment of a dream a freefall out of time
travelling in this plane I trace my journey
the one I have travelled many times

Many times through the gentle strains
that seep through to the sensual being
I have felt giddiness divorced from the flesh

Many times I have travelled home
unwrapped from flesh and happy at being helpless
drifting in a coal black night to the beginning

Now I travel in this devouring flesh
and sense the rough the smooth the grit the gravel
the heat permeating through the pores

The mind fragments as colours entwine themselves
floating through clouds changing their hue
and thudding back bright reflecting the sun

I see my blue blue sky with my brown brown eyes
I smell fear the bitterness of departure
I smell the earth and know that I am coming home

Cape Flats

Blue skies and the bright sun
cannot defeat the vision of shanty towns
stretching out into the landscape.

This is where the green grass of youth
and the faded flowers of age
cannot see the dream of the new day.

In a dialect of this flat landscape
speaking through dust, they tell us that,
the only thing that grows is trouble.

In a stillborn dream of freedom,
sharp-eyed faces of the unemployed
do a dance of survival.

The leaders, troubled and bewildered
are scurrying back to old positions
while the young demand a new revolution.

The sell-by date for change has gone,
some call on the ghost that went before,
and animals are reborn in the form of humans.

We hear the Hyenas laughing at death,
see Baboons scrambling over problems,
hear eagled evangelists praying for more,
see Springboks leaping to avoid bullets, and
watch the white Jackal beady eyed and dangerous.

The wind and red dust devoid of subtlety
blow uncertainty, while he,

    The prodigal son sits on the step,
    Smoking and falling out of time:
    Flying birdlike and way out of mind.

As he listens to the frog's phlegm-throated croak
he sees the knife-flicking forked tongue.
Now on his back he hears the crik, crik, chorus
of night Crickets making strange warped legends.

Crabs living in houses protected by 'Armed Guard
Response', ignore threats of death,
as they hide under the sunlight of self-delusion.

Come Again

Let me describe to you
the open space.
The place of brown soil
the mountain peaks.

Soft mud,
between the toes, clings
to the mind.
I was there where the song bird sings

You know,
I was there touching
the water,
where pebbles grow from molten mass.

Picking
smooth round pebbles
soaked
in mystery hiding a bone in stone.

With mumbo jumbo mysteries
fossilising human endeavour

Handling
the hidden heritage
immersed
in history's secret inscriptions.

Touching
a brain drained of imagination
trying to sell,
to tell of a fear it does not know.

A body
drunk with information,
and ravenous for more
staggers blindly without shame of foreboding,

towards the sensual earth
that bore it and one day will consume it.

ARIANA TIKAO

Trail of Tyrants

We tread the trails of Napoleon
We tread the trails of William
We read a plaque that here Harold met his end
royal blood spilling from arrow-pierced crown
sandy-faced Abbey an edifice or brag
depending on whose side of the moat you're on

And now, wilding meadows spread
bees hover and alight on yellow
hawkbit and purple self-heal blooms
busy in their attempt to remain

Our species—not so smart.
We keep on Fighting
We keep on Hating
We keep on Forgetting
erasing those who would remember
Poets. Scholars. Orators
rendered mute
like women
as chattels

We walk along the straight canal to Rye
feeling the spasmodic warmth of the sun
hearing the intermittent buzz of insects
trampling the sienna mud that also clung
to the boots of legions

ANNE ROUSE

Fling

Hello, darling. I was proud of that.
(A year had passed,
the visitation felt abrupt.)
A hose stream eddied down
Ashburnham Hill;
ran coldly on, relentlessly ad-hoc.
The families toiled up from
the church school.
I heard your answering voice
above a lorry's sliding bass,
its gruffest note, sustained.
What oscillates, is us.

Return to Sender

It's a no man's land: rusted side gate,
gully of last year's leaves and briars,
grey aureoles of seeding dandelion—sentinels
against the neighbours' stucco and rose.

I wait here for the greetings to wash over me.
A moth beats, flimsy, against the entry light.
Brown water rots in the terrace's troughs and urns.
I can smell its marshy stagnancy.

Then I'm like the prodigal's brother, railing
at the vines, *why's this layabout, death, so welcome here?*
I go to the feast, eventually, and wonder
at the conjurors, their daylight getaway.

They sweep out, their sequinned trains trailing
in the rutted driveway, to the wooded road
—as love, like a stooping bodyguard,
walks with them to the end.

Heel

Roaming Sedlescombe fields,
near Battle—no lark or corncrake
hereabouts in 30 years—the heel dips,
betrayed: a subaltern, badly booted.

Thetis with the hair like wheat, grasps
her newborn's foot; dangles him headlong,
blue, dipped into deathless Styx.
He'll leave his sandalled crescent arc

on foreign sands. Diva, fate's coming for you.
A tenpence blister scrapes right off,
a raw heart in the heel, palpitating to the chug
of the haymaker back-combing the field:

stubble, heel traps,
under its hefty black ridged tires,
its scrambling blade-edge,
the grasses overthrown.

Uncertain Ode

This is safe water—a bedroom striped
with twilight. I'm adrift in the cave's mouth,
relaying white words of the moon.
They're emptying the flat next door.
All her things are going: silver brushes,
ormulu, porcelain terrier, throaty hullo.

Reviewing the day's accidents:
a blaze on the railings, amassed clouds.
The light works free, is barred again
by (apparent) immensities.
(You're not untouched, it concerns you,
you will be wanted).

Hope

Hope Floats.
A shit film with Sandra Bullock,
    from 1998 which you could only remember
because it sounded like Coke float,
a scoop of vanilla ice cream
    bouncing in cola's brown fizz,
making it creamy cold
    as it slips down your throat,
        but warming, comforting,
  making you feel everything is okay, even though your
  teeth
are in decay.
Fluffy froth stuck to the glass, like the gold froth
        on the black waves, which screamed
            as they hit the rocks outside Belfast that February.
    And his arms were around your waist.
Now, each mid-day, you and him walk to the sea
        your little boy strapped to your chest.
You hope for other things these days,
for things bigger than you.
And sometimes you think
you see it—hope
flickering, twitching in the seat
where the sky and sea meet.
Maybe it does float.

Jane Midwinter at Fairlight Country Park

Real Boy

My fiancée calls me Pinocchio.
And we laugh
because we both know the story.
I lit a fire.
I made the whale sneeze,
but somehow got snagged on a tooth.
They say that a boy
needs to roll in the ashes
before he can be a man.
I'm still finding soot in pleats
and embers in breast pockets.
Sometimes when I speak to people
I get nervous.

Nervous of judgement,
of being inadequate.

But then I notice a trail
of dust behind them
and I know
I'm not alone.

My therapist said I

        should try
writing my
thoughts
down

I told him I've been
Writing my thoughts down
As long as I can remember

My therapist said I

        should try not
writing my
thoughts
down

Avalanche

I can't fault a single person
for their actions

For I know that our actions
aren't our own

You can't have a movement
without traction

And you can't blame
a landslide on one stone

Ember

When our dreams burn
and we dance
in the ashes

Be light—
As an ember in flight
And keep moving

Absolutely

Prone to pedantry—
I find problems in the predicate

When Nietzsche said

There are no absolutes

He sounded pretty definite

HARRY LEBOWSKI

i saw the blue moon of august 19th 2024 from hastings shores

the light of the
once in a
blue moon

pierces through the skin of pregnant clouds

like an ultrasound
i can see the life in
nimbus belly

before waters break on fertile ground

OLI SPLEEN

Mother & the Spoon

At times, tormented by the tones
Of memories and mobile phones
Encased and cut-off in my room
The walls and windows my cocoon

I'd lie in linen streaked with mud
And filter poison through my blood
Letting the languorous hours slide
Out of the spoon, lain at my side

All time would slip beneath me then
Distorting space and vision
As if bobbed upon my ocean
Summoned softly by its moon

I'd be cradled by the currents
And the waters would not drown me
They'd just gently wrap around me
With the warmness of the womb

As hours passed, the haze would clear
A voice of shame resounding near
As, time-to-time, my gaze would fall
To mother's picture on the wall

Which gazed right back as if to say
"Dear child don't throw your life away
Don't wallow in your septic pit
Of filth, depravity and shit"

With gnawing guilt, inadequacy
White worms which writhe inside of me
I'd smoke a fag and have a drink
And hurt my head trying not to think

I'd gaze at mother, then the spoon
Then let my candle bathe the room
Letting its golden fingers lick
And cook myself another fix

Mother you're fading faster now
Disjointed from my vision
As I'm swept away on currents
Cloying for my every breath

My childhood's but a memory
Mere glimpses of euphoria
That flood in waves and then cascade
Down to my deepest depths

Mother you're fading faster now
Disjointed from my vision
As I'm swept away on currents
Gasping for my every breath

My childhood now is but a memory
Mere glimpses of euphoria
That flood in waves and then cascade
Down to my deepest depths

Almost Young

When I was an old man
Many moons ago
Regrets and fears would cloud my years
I had no space to grow

But now the clouds are parting
It feels like spring has sprung
I'm learning how to live life
And I'm nearly almost young

Life is what we make it
I'll contribute my verse
And extract inspiration
From all things I can't reverse

There's feasts that must be tasted
And songs that should be sung
Let me embrace not waste it
Now I'm nearly almost young

And as we play the game of life
We find it's not so fair
'Cause though we fight with all our might
It seems we go nowhere

And as we climb the ladders
We find snakes on every rung
A slide to the inevitable
Ending that must come

So when I'm on my deathbed
Be it near or far away
I hope I will have few regrets
Blown chances, wasted days

'Cause we're only here so briefly
As we satellite a sun
Whose rays give light and life
So we may learn to become young

The Garden

Once I dreamed of a garden
Whose fountains brimmed with wine
Whose emerald hills and pastures rolled
With fruit on every vine

Whose swans were white as ivory
Whose harvests ripe and sweet
For all around these beauteous grounds
Exquisite things to eat

With the wine came inspiration
And the food enriched my soul
A great future stretched before me
And I ran and reached each goal

And my soul was high on dreaming
And my heart knew only love
A great future stretched before me
And the sky was bright above

But now the soil is poisoned
And the fountain swims with blood
And the swans' necks all lay broken
Amongst the rotting food

And the sky is thick with darkness
And the plants know only night
And have wilted in the winter
At the dying of the light

For my soul is cold and wretched
And my heart knows only hate
And has hardened to a boulder
Of a tremendous weight

Now the poison's my addiction
I have frightened all my friends
My soul was once a garden
But all summers end

Still Life

I'll paint a still life
A still life
There is still life in me yet
Just to capture light and fill life
With what light I can reflect

To preserve a frozen moment
To remember, not forget
In a riot of radiant colour
With the paint all wild and wet

When once my dreams would yield the freshest fruit
Kaleidoscopes of brilliant flowers bloomed
But then a blight descended and took root
My still life decomposing, all aspirations doomed

Now, awaking from this nightmare
Of missed chances and regret
I find my heart still beating
My body drenched in sweat

I've lived a wretched ill life
With death's ever looming threat
So let me paint a still life
There is still life in me yet

And whilst these fruits lose freshness every day
As every day I grow a little older
Still there is worth and wisdom in decay
Oh see my still life ripen
Watch it blossom bright with mould

If my fate has not unfolded
And my path is still not set
I can find a way to will life
To the place I need to get

I must nurture life, not kill life
Free my soul of every debt
I'll paint a still life
A still life
There is still life in me...

Plans One, Two and Three

We were planning to meet
In the secluded café of a dream
But the beating males,
Eyes blinded by drunken headlights,
Waved a threat between pain and goodbye,
One shout late; the sleeper
Woke to a white wound,
Breathing out floating sheets
Over last night's missing,
Tired faces receding into downs and outs.

We were planning to meet
In the deserted office of a smile;
But the swindling players,
Hopes numbered in tens of thousands,
Drove a wedge between rain and exit,
Two hearts long; the schemer
Fled in a fine flame,
Signing on floppy discs,
For last night's warning,
Weary futures retreating into scores and wins.

We were planning to meet
In the neglected hotel of a wish;
But the glittering children,
Singing in treacherous keys,
Moved a block between gain and decay,
Three tears thick; the searcher
Left in a low line,
Crouching by coughing walls,
For last night's taxi,
Sagging features resolving into wheels and deals

Cars

When I walked the cold roads
Of the winter night
I loved and envied the cars;
Wanted to sit in them,
Heater whirring warmly gently
With someone I knew
Who was nameless, in love;
And waking warm in the
Sunsilvered morning
In my small home,
Drive into the sharp fresh sunlight
Of a new and wilder love

Endless Room

The endless room
Where first loves
Are discussed in whispers
May be dusty
But among the spiders'
Idea cobwebs
People still live in summer
"Even the drugs
have not been consistent
since those green leaves",
She says
And the old songs
Arnold Layne See Emily Play My
White Bicycle
Still hold their starry meanings
While the new are often
Mothfashions that brush
At windows, faces.
The room is anywhere
And we, anyone.
Why should we know
Who we are, go anywhere,
Move outside
Into places of cruelty
Forced to commit harm
With clown ambitions
Under nightfalls.
The endless room
Stretches into sun
The holidays not packaged
But out of control
Unscheduled flights
Through desert jungle London
nights

Endless somewhere
Room of summer
Nights of never
Knowing where the next
Dusty loves
Discussed in echo
Chambers burning
Midnight blue
Midnight new
Lamps of old

THERESA SULLIVAN

To the Fisherman

Should necessity be in the forming crowd
to turn around and wander by
thinking of long forgotten waves
of talking winds that speak no change
of children singing while the lilies died
hands adjoined in a circle formed
    though the lilies died
    though the lilies died
yet the sea shall not yield up her sons.

Should the sons of the sea
have gone down in the deep
darkened, like memories dead
we'd still have danced round the Maypole
    amidst the waterfall
while light wove about us her tapestry of blue.
Though the children sing the lilies are dead
though the children sing the lilies are dead
yet the sea shall not yield up her sons.

Little Bo Peep

They took the child
from out her arms
she knew they would you see
"She's touched," they said,
"Sick in the head.
Mad as mad can be."

Little Bo Peep
lost her sheep
all on a summer day,
three blind mice came
and took the same
they whisked her all away.

They took her child
they took her rights
she knew they would, you see.
She lost all will
she grew quite still
as sad as sad can be.

Little Bo Peep
lost her sheep
all on a summer day,
three blind mice came
and took the same
they whisked her all away.

NAOMI WOOD

Dried Roses

Isn't it funny how roses
Do that?
Blooming ebullient in bowls of light
Until we decide to discard their beauty?
Wise women
Know the secret.
That, they only go
And form
A delicate sculpture
Of their brittle bones,
Twist their heads
To whisper and clot their pigment.
Crystallising
To make light and depth
Of their own architecture.
Doing what it takes
To live again.

PETE DONOHUE

marlon in the window

marlon sits
behind the wide window
of a boutique bar
& eatery

slipping irish whiskey
from his own bottle
into his latest
pint of guinness
in full view
of all who pass
along this cobbled
pedestrian zone

benches & tables
outside the window
throng with smokers
cigarettes spliffs & vapes

all the locals
know his story
the passing trade
don't give a toss

marlon eyes
the smokers enviously
gulping guinness
to soothe his pain
he can't remember
the last time he paid
for any drink
in this beautiful bar

his tab is kept
constantly topped up
by friends & lovers
even enemies
no one else uses

marlon's chair
out of respect
for his final days

marlon sits
behind the wide window
his remembrance portrait
artistically framed.

gin boy joe & the illuminated g-string

he saw god
in everything that flashed
before his eyes
how do you think i got here
he asked
pointing out three ufos
that bookended & spined
the bluesky streak
of a swerving paintbrush
signing off
another hastings winter
in stained satsuma
sunset

taking my hand
like it was all he had left
to hold onto
kissing my knuckles
through nicotine moustache
underlining
his frosted beard
to taste
that metallic taint
of keith richards skull ring
swimming in sweet sweat
of managed withdrawal
on the twitch
of my bishop finger
he said
remember the days
we jammed together
between whiskey bottles
when butler's gap
was still boarded up
& he fingered his treasure
a battered guitar

acquired through serendipity
by paying off
cocaine debts
for a former desperado
as if i could ever forget

look at the sky
he laughed
now it was dark
& airplane lights
flashed their schadenfreude
whilst smugglers' lamps
flickered in decoy
there's a g-string up there
he reminded me
& although it wasn't obvious
i gave him the benefit
of the doubt
& to be fair
he was probably right
all along.

badgers & foxes

it's not like london
down here at the seaside
not so many cops
not so many cameras
not so many prying eyes
but the interest is still here
for the white & the brown
& the money too
ill gained or kosher
so demand increases
& supply follows suit
as he sits on his bench
this dreadlocked yardie
at the narrow steep path
from the corner of the hill
down to the old town
behind the allotments
modelling the grand old duke
halfway up
& halfway down
like his customers
conducting his business
in the woodland strip
laid out in a badger hole
no one can catch him
it's all planned out
the deals go down
the cash accumulates
until that day
the local wildlife
get the better of him
& the badgers & foxes
have some party
beneath their own
hunter's blue moon.

NICK WEBB

Tin Cans

I get used to their bloom.
The places they're found
The joy they bring.
A tunnel escape for the voiceless opera
I get used to the blues
of their fading spectrum.
Flight wreckage from a budget airline never cleared
I get used to the way they held hope for so many answers
offered none, but just enough for one more.

And one more.

SUSAN J LELLIOTT

Winter Worms

Do not be mistook or mistaken.
In the Norwegian-like half-light,
We are not talking *death* death.
Under budded fists on the deep red Dogwood,
Where you cannot look,
Six feet under,
Worms turn in lubricious circles.

TIM BARLOW

The Horsepower of Love

He's cleaning his Cortina's carburettor,
and trying to fix his fragile four-stroke heart;
his partner says their love life could be better—
the diagnostics show that they will part.

Whatever revved them up before has gone;
he used to serenade her with a sonnet.
Now feats of engineering turn him on—
he gets his kicks from underneath the bonnet,

where pistons pump in cylinders of steel
each time he puts his foot down to the floor.
It makes him feel the way he wants to feel:
secure. Motors won't walk out the door.

Machines won't break your heart, like people can;
he prefers life as a petrosexual man.

Just Coming Up to Our Finest

We're just coming up to our finest time
A tipping point, somewhere between
The work that we've done and the fun that's to come
We're neither too grey or too green

We're mature in the mind and young in the heart
We're just coming up to our finest
The snow-covered peaks are now clearly in view
The climb is mostly behind us

We carry no guilt, we're not burdened by fear
We know what we do and don't like
We're just coming up to our finest time
The graphs of our lives will soon spike

Come and sit down at this table with us
Bring us your smiles and the wine list
Let's show our loved ones who cannot be here
We're just coming up to our finest

DAVE ARNOLD

On Your Birthday You Can Do Anything

You can stand on your head
You can jump out of bed
Ride a horse upside down
You can fly around town

Have your dinner for breakfast
Or your supper for tea
You can be Father Christmas
You can even be me!

You can fly a kite on the ground
While you are up in the air
You can even say, No!
When you really mean, Yeah!

You can suck a blancmange
Whole through a straw
You can even eat jelly
Off a wobbly floor

All these things on your birthday
Are for you to do
But don't tell anyone
I told you to!

MARTIN HONEYSETT

Bees

Why do Bees
Have bandy knees
Why don't their legs grow straight?
Is it that
They're much too fat
And their legs can't bear the weight?
Is there a disease
Which affects bee's knees
Or is it simply fate?

Fernando the Frog

At jumping, Fernando the Frog was good,
He jumped much further than other frogs could.

In the morning he jumped out of bed,
He would hit the ceiling with his head.

Fernando could jump the pond in one hop,
While the others got halfway and went plop.

But all that jumping made him so thin,
That one day he jumped right out of his skin.

He didn't jump much at all after that,
But just sat around and got rather fat.

If you see a frog who's tubby and bare,
It's poor Fernando with no skin to wear.

Kevin the Kangaroo

Kevin was a Kangaroo,
Who dearly loved his mother,
He used to sit inside her pouch,
Along with Bruce, his brother.

But mother took such giant hops,
To get from place to place,
That many times the little lads,
Were thrown out on their face.

They went to see their grandad,
To find out what to do.
He could always sort out problems,
Such a clever Kangaroo.

Grandad got some seatbelts,
From an old car on the dump,
And fitted them in mother's pouch,
When she landed from a jump.

So then there was no problem,
For when mother leapt around,
The boys were strapped inside her pouch,
All nicely safe and sound.

DELLA REYNOLDS

Good Sport!

Wanna get across the line Babe?
I'm sure you know the score.
You can call the shots Babe,
My gloves are off for sure.
Don't give me a hard time now,
The ball is in your court
I can go the distance
I'm teed up and I'm taut.
You knocked me out the park Babe,
When you said there's no holds barred,
But you stumped me with your curve ball,
I was blind-sided so hard.
You were my sparring partner,
But you hit below the belt,
I tried to block and tackle,
As I went down for the count.
I was hoping for a slam dunk,
To take one for the team,
But I need to pass the baton
Now I'm running out of steam.
I guess I'll throw the towel in,
Gonna take an early bath,
You think that it's all over...
But there's still the second half.
When the two of us play hard ball
On my home turf sticky wicket
You can have the upper hand Babe,
All's fair in love and cricket.
I'm looking for an easy win.
The home stretch is in sight,
You're bound to lose your shirt Babe.
'Cause it's kicking off tonight.

STEVE TASANE

Hastings is

a storm and a rainbow,
grey and scary, crashing loudly,
but when the black clouds part
the pavements glisten and the sun shines proudly.

Hastings is a brand new school jumper
that does not yet fit.
You can't wait to grow into it.
Hastings is cold chips
picked from the plate that's been dumped by the sink
because you just can't help it.

Hastings is a brand new bike,
zooming along the prom, splashing through puddles,
taking you any place you like.

Hastings is an old rocking chair
made from wood, pulled from the low tide
carved and varnished with care.

Hastings is a smelly old dog with big yellow teeth
that tries to lick your face and give you fleas
and likes to have its belly rubbed although it's caked in mud.

Hastings is the supermarket where you once got lost,
and the corner shop with the man at the counter who
    laughs a lot.

Hastings is a snapped branch, a play-sword.
Hastings is PSP. You never get bored.

It is where TV was discovered and where time grows old.
Hastings is a battle. It is the centre of your world.

Battle Rap

"I'm King Harold and I can channel
a marching army from battle to battle.
The storming Normans ignored my warnings
so my war men are swarming now the day is dawning.
We won't let the horde in, breeching our borders.
We'll kick them into touch, disarray and disorder,
deliver them a battering, send them scattering.
The rabble will be clamouring to get back to the Channel
when we've given them a hammering.
The Frenchman's henchmen aren't too tough to mention—
all that Ooh la la is losing our attention,
camped in tents with deadly intention,
sharpening their arrows, ratcheting the tension,
sticking their oar in, waging war in the hope it's rewarding.
But it's seaside suicide, they're in deep water
like whales that are beached, or cattle to the slaughter.
We'll battle to the bitter end, exactly as we ought to."

"I'm William The First, thirsting for trouble,
mess with me, I'm gonna burst your bubble.
I'll attack the Saxons, batter their shields,
axe the battalions in the battlefield.
We'll dominate the drama, shatter their armour,
leave them weeping for their sheep and crying for their Mama.
Over-the-hill-Harold ought to throw in the towel.
I'll have that sadsack Saxon right over a barrel,
cos I'm William the Conqueror, totally superior,
scarier than a pit-bull terrier tearing up the area.
I'll pillage all your apples, put a boot up your posterior.
You'll never evade us, we're invincible invaders.
This is the field where you're gonna get slayed
as down in the valley, we lay waiting
to lay waste Harold in the Battle of Hastings.
He's gonna get one in the eye. Listen to him cry,
see him going down before I seize his crown,
cos my name is William, I'm notorious.
They call me the Conqueror cos I'm totally victorious."

Salena Godden on the Fire Hills

The Kipper

It wasn't the galley
My own hell of smells—
Pots sliding, see-saw fashion
From one end of the range to the other
Discharging their dubious cargo onto the hotplate
Giving a stench that mingled with the constant backdrop
of diesel oil
Nor was it the pitch and toss as the bows strained to clear
the waters
Or the roll, as the sky gave way to sea, rolling back to sky—
Was it then a secret fear that this was not
Simply normal Atlantic weather?
No! It was the kipper what done it!
Suspended from the deck above
Swinging before my face and
Amid cruel laughter
That caused
In one
Fluid
Motion
The loss
Of both
My dignity
And my breakfast

Nature's Highway (a la David Attenborough)

Black snake,
Laying as if discarded
Racoon,
Camouflaged against the black top
Skunk,
Blending to the white line
Deer,
Sleeping, never to waken
Pedestrian,
Last of its species, perhaps
Timidly
Daring to cross the road

He will beat you
with a thousand words
to turn your head into the wind

He will open your soul
and bleed you
like the apothecary's leach

And yet you will turn to him
in the quiet of the night
to see if he sleeps
or hungers

JANE MIDWINTER

scattered pins

why did you tell me now
for years i doubted then
one night i saw the
dirty tanker spilling
muck and heard its filthy
polluting lies but

why did you tell me now
that's where you went
those nights i thought i knew
but lie you did about fresh air
to lighted windows for that
was i not soft enough

why did you tell me now
the fabric's almost sewn
the lining smoothed the pins removed
your waistcoat trimmed
so handsome thin
tall lies my husband lies

why did you tell me now
as i had lit the wick
as we began to dance
your trembling hand
that touched or
did we dance too close

why did you tell me now
that silence couldn't be
you had to open up
you couldn't keep it shut
the windows shut the door
couldn't let that silence speak

why did you tell me now

Wave Ghazal

This boy is in love with Maria
He wears a wedding ring on the wrong finger

Satellite dishes scan the troposphere
For voices warm with promise

When he finishes the fighting
He is going to Belgrade to marry her

The industrial palaces are crumbling
Voices die mutate their rays

Of dark intentionality flicker resonate
In blood bone muscle in the cathedrals

On the floor of his truck
His Kalashnikov points into the trees

Too many voices call mutate the duende
In the quantum void

The convoy's trucks clatter through the forest
On a mountain road he hears

The duende's long bow wave
On the receiving station

And somewhere there's a house
Made of blond wood filmed with dust

The spirit in that house the
Spiral in the dust

They Didn't Go Home

The poets and their entourages, appendages,
readerships, theoretical props and absences
are variously and severally assembled.
A shows pictures and reads the words.
B takes seriously the notations in cowboy comic balloons.
C vacillates, and comes down on the side of externality.
D demonstrates conviviality (again).
E emphasises the smallness of the audience.
F is quiet and has with him a pair of rollerblades.
G, as usual, enigmatic.
H waxes shaven.
I have had my hair newly cut but have forgotten about it.
Sound travels from the street below because it is a warm
    night & there is
no reason for the folks to go home.

Like

My love is like

          Oh no it isn't

And its loss is like

          For heaven's sake

Like, what if it were all a
big mistake?

          Because you're jealous & so
          judgemental

You can't talk to me like that
what can I say

          Because you have some
          personal opera going on

Its music, what, huge
like a locomotive
imaged at strange resolutions

          No   Nothing like that

It's too luminous a conceit?

          It's enough to change the
          shape of a man's head

It hurts like fuck
it hurts my like, human heart
you know what I mean

I mean nothing is like anything else*

* This line is stolen from Eric Mottram. Something always to bear
in mind.

A Dream of Reclaimed Land

Time knows it   equivalence knows it
the filth know it   mine host behind the bar
knows it   the helix of language knows it
surplus value knows it   the boys who
take care of these things know it
Mary Quite Contrary, the twin strikers, the midnighters
all know it   Trace who is 4 Gary knows it
numbers melody mayhem & transformation know it

But you my beauty who find yourself in a place
vastly crammed with incident and resource, and see
no way out of it, you do not know it.
You venture onto "reclaimed land" but it's dark to you:

Ahead, huge buildings with screens on which luminous text
Scrolls & forever transforms, yet seems hardly to change.

Naomi Wood walking down from the West Hill

U have to read to write good

So sometimes I like to read
And go into their dreams
I feel the grass like the wind
In Dylan Thomas and everything
Smells of semen he's always
Talking about salt and ears
Of corn and things I hear his
Deep voice imagine Welsh
Baritone or just booming or
Hungry and dripping with words

And then I go on hobartpulp.com
To see tens of unique but similar
Tales of realisation, family, love
The new poetry and I look over old
Couture Noir feature lists and
Maybe I write something in LA or
Miami and then it's vagabondcitylit
If they've decided to do an issue
Lately and I'm looking for poems
About transgressional romances

On my table are two Hunter Thompson
Collections I read over and over
And three collections by local
Poets Andrew Graves and Penny
Pepper and Society of the Spectacle
And a horn and a clay jug and my
Almost broken headphones taped
Together with hairbands and a pot
Of coffee and as I get to the peak
Of the coffee high my mouth vents
Petrol and I roll my head back.

I, Adrienne

The uniform is important, the raiment,
the drapery, my skirt/ is a way of being,/
my knickers are part of what define me
Even though I look out over a goddess
in(of?) grassy hills and long/for the naked touch
of leaves on my skin, / I lie in forest beds
and notice foxcubs and woodpeckers
Here this ruffled cloth and some unseen band
Make me
In front of them I don't know or care
much too much
the insolence of skin still becomes poison
As the sun sets over bodies
And my pack panic rises
Our other animals have fur and thicknesses.
Ruminate quietly in fields,
Waiting for death.
We have freedom to fear
and tremble in petticoats.

Don't equate me

The same Grammarly ad five times 25 minutes
The same grammarly ad ten times an hour
25 miles of grammarly source code can't
tell me that inconsistent capitals, no full stops
random line breaks, can't tell me
How to improve lazy and bleeding noise—
Is a cover up: 6 times twenty five, 150 empty
grammarly ads for air heads who are acting in ads
School never let them write
Like this
And 25 maths questions about fruit doesn't
Tell you how an apple tastes in 10mph wind
On the seashore, salt-sodden trousers and dying
Devices in the pebbles and health among the
Broken glass paraphernalia of cutting and honest
Forced out phrases with hyphens in the wrong places.

PAUL A GREEN

Statement

Our privateering time ships are beyond control. We crashed through the universe like swollen dodgems. My cells are flickering. I'm a hive of dancing zeros.

In the blackness of a hole we eat light, breaking into a Kosmos that's gone wrong, to become notorious sightings, streaking across the screen grabs of weary officers in Siberia, Northwood, Iron Mountain. We are the new aliens, falling like a rain of toads, bursting into a flare of pixels.

Dark matter clogs the starscape. The disasters are flying overhead like large angels. Shrivel into yourselves. Space worms have timed out. We are boxed into the body and its ticking clock...

The Rain

What signal is being communicated in the rain? No fancy in the flux of water, these molecules licking through the air, smearing their halo over and all around, to liquidate the syntax of vision in visions—it's all suggestive—"know what I mean?"

In the rain the thing is. The thing is that flutter of water that flattens the rank grass, out there, out front. Like all pleasures in the wet hedges, it's a tiny incandescent thing. You know. All about the rain.

We like the recurrence of rain, the soft pattern, its grey beat. No shame in admitting a preference for tree dwelling "entirely surrounded by water". We're in. It's out.

But that isn't the whole signal. A reading of the rain goes (and grows) well beyond that. The rain states that the swimming of small lights, the drench of fallen stars, what we fabricate in darts and glances, all that—and you know what I mean— is, simply, the right forest to pick ferns in.

Bed Time

It must have happened on a railway, but direct-injection memory has failed, only a few words left. Let me rearrange them, please.

The train slumbered along. It was the anniversary of winter. We were awash with night. The hooded stranger in blue slept across the opposite seat, face in hiding. He was dreaming of a meat factory, a mouse dump, a coil spring holding back the horror of the world, a room clanking with menaces, tinned soup splashing breasts, fried viscera, lost ships? All attempts at telepathic linkage failed. As passengers uncrinkled sweet papers, my powers of spelling became uncertain... He moved at last, woken by my concentration, and rose, to open a bag and settle down with Newsweek.

The snoring diesels were moving me too slowly. I was re-running into memory, just to keep me going: headscarf, green check skirt, black sweater, suede coat. I was touched by her glee, her small hands, her sweet music.

I was dreaming my way towards a bed, another night train.

Eleventh Hour

In the eleventh hour of the poem
I found the first word. It screamed
like burnt metal, a bad spell

In the second second of the poem
I misspelt the word, a cry
from a hot heart, bad metaphor
for loves lost in the landline

In the first three minutes of the bursting poem
I broke a word, a hot shout out
for the lost boys and girls
crying in their metal cells

On the last day of the poem
I had to have the last word
the word of hearts
lost in all the hours

Greenie

As soon as we left it, the wild began.
Our plough-shares slit the umbilical,
Severed the song-lines, so the booming bane
Of guilt summoned the gulls, their gall
Mocking the plovers' wit, the curlew
Calling for meadowy chaos to somehow forgive you.
And the wind blasts open our door, wilder
Now than my screen-saver crags, wilder
Still than smart Alecx the AI scarecrow,
Who exhumes gold from the GM rainbow,
Whisking it up to some stray satellite
And, wildest of all, weeding that starry night
For our space-junk selfie.

Trust the Process

What does that even mean? *Just write what you do,*
how you get there. Do what? Get where?
I felt I was being led down a path with no garden.
F'instance?
That last one you wrote, how did that happen?
Hmm, I thought, is this trickery or a genius question?
Thinking back I'd:
1. Got two notebooks out of the bin
an ipad and half a pencil that needed sharpening.
2. Opened the door to the milkman who was ranting
about cows rampaging in the high street.
3. Made a gallon of good Cuban coffee (you know, to get me
in the mood).
Interesting, she said, *but irrelevant to the process.*
Process, process, did she mean:
4. That line I'd read out at breakfast about the mountain of
chicken heads being amassed under EU rules.
5. The fact that I had definitely got out the wrong side of
the bed.
6. That freewrite about a murderous Little Red Riding Hood
outfoxing the wolf.
7. The discarded ideas stuck on post-it notes over the front
of the back door.
Now you're getting somewhere, she said, collecting
the way-markers and taking them with her.

from Dwelling

seagape

seaanchor

seaash

seaasphodel

seaaster

seaattack

seaawe

seababel

seabait

seabalanced

seabank

seabar

seabased

seabat

seabathed

seabeam

seabear

seabeast

seabeaten

seabecalmed

seabed

seabees

seabeggar

seabeing

seabell

seabelt

seabent

seabind

seabird

seabitten

seablackened

seabladder

seablast

seabled

seablessed

seablight

seablind

seablink

seablithe

seablitz

seabloom

seablown

seablue

seablur

seaboard

seabook

seaboot

seaborer

                              seaborder

                                    seaborn

                              seabottle

                        seabottom

                  seabounded

            seabrace

      seabranch

seabreach

      seabread

            seabred

                  seabrief

                        seabright

                              seabrink

                                    seabrim

                              seabroken

                        seabuilt

CONQUEST

Templehead. If you do feel someone behind you, it's your
eyes. I should have begun these researches much earlier. It's
the only way. The temperature is raised to room, or decays,
as the context demands. The colour is fluorescent orange.
I'm not altogether comfortable with how this is unravelling.
We've been allotted a minimum of three lines to each
expansion. The smell of burning stubble spread from the
surrounding countryside. Until you have read this, nothing
will become clear.

HELP

I want to re-enter the medieval mind. All the local electricity is directed straight through me. To detonate you must turn the key clockwise by ninety degrees. It's unclear how all the instructions knit together. There are intervening obstacles. (I need somebody.) I once lost all sense of time but later regained it. A breath of wind emerges from the horizon, a pillar of light.

IMRAM

It's about one of their submarines, isn't it. I woke to find myself back on the island. The hero is a number of the dynasty. Some objects are highly radioactive. He meets otherworldly creatures. These need neither the excitation of light nor the stimulus of electricity. Finally he returns to his native land. On route there's a collision with an antique trireme. (Picture a type of bold face with lineaments of equal thickness.) Being but a pitiful vessel, it sinks. Crew is expendable.

INEVITABLE

The whole shebang. They were rearranged in alphabetic order. This darkens the waters and conceals the pursuit. He writes in relatively short sustained bursts (a secular inventory). Every day we're counted in and counted out. Who is this man being described before us? There are less than one hundred remaining. Some have wondered about the sequence in this argument. Some say he must have mixed up the pages on the way to the printer.

THE MOON

Logomachy. Close all the hatches behind me. I'm never coming back.

JUDITH SHAW

A marriage

You are in the garden.
You ask him to take
the other end of the wet sheet.
You hold, he twists.

The water pours
on the crazy paving.
The weeds grow faster.
The woman from next door

strolls round the back,
ignoring him to give you
a huge bunch of folded
tea towel lilies.

You drop the sheet
in the dirt and kiss her.
Behind you, four elephants,
fig branches in their trunks,

hum The Arrival of the Queen of Sheba.
Their tablecloth wings
lift them over the house
and out of view.

The Towel

My mother was always afraid of losing her marbles.
I'd imagine a black suede drawstring pouch on a red tiled floor,
coloured marbles rolling around. There's a scene in the camp
from *Coup de Foudre* before the mother of the film-maker

agrees to marry the guard. She thinks he is a gentile
and only finds out he's Jewish at the registration
when he gives his names: Mordecai Simon Korski
and there's a moment she doesn't know what to do,

but marries him anyway and of course they do survive
otherwise the film-maker wouldn't have been born,
and nothing is shown in the film about all the others who don't,
before all of that there's a scene in the camp where the mother

of the film-maker is drying her hair with a clean white towel
and somehow when I think of how my crazy grandmother
died in Gurs, it gets overlaid with this clean white towel
which I don't believe but is printed on my memory as if it were true.

In this poem my mother

is lying on a blanket beneath an oak tree,
a picnic spread on a white tablecloth.

She pillows her head on her hands, watches the light
dapple through the leaves. Soon her husband

will stroll to join her but for now she's enjoying
being alone. She has no pain between her shoulder blades,

her mother is still alive, her grandmother died
gently, her friends are neither dead nor scattered.

She is not afraid she left the front door open
or the tap turned on. She is not afraid she undercooked

the chicken and poisoned her family, nor
that driving home last night she ran someone over

and didn't realise it. In this poem
she simply delights in the sunshine.

ORNA ROSS

Recalling Brigid

Queen of queens, they called her
in the old books, the Irish Mary.
Never washed her hands, nor her head
in sight of a man, never looked
into a man's face. She was good
with the poor, multiplied food,
gave ale to lepers. Among birds,
call her dove; among trees, a vine.
A sun among stars.

Such was the sort of woman
preferred as the takeover was made:
consecrated cask, throne to His glory,
intercessor.

Brigid said nothing to any of this,
the reverence, or the upbraidings.
Her realm is the lacuna,
silence her sceptre,
her own way of life its own witness.

Out of desire, the lure of lust
or the dust of great deeds,
she was distorted:
to consort, mother-virgin,
to victim or whore.

I am not as womanly
a woman as she.
So I say: Let us see.
Let us say how she is the one.

It is she who conceives
and she who does bear.
She who knitted us in the womb
and who will cradle our tomb-fraying.

Daily she offers her arms,
clothes us in compassion,
smiles as we wriggle
for baubles.

Yes, it is she who lifts you aloft
to whisper through your ears,
to kiss your eyes,
to touch her cooling
cheek to your cheek.

Nowruz Mubarak?

Maybe it's the disconnect. At the wheel,
he enjoys a series of green-lit traffic lights,
smoothly cruising through smooth roads

sad, but also amused at himself: an alien
alienated. Is this about exile? He was connected,
part of a new generation creating a new nation

from the ruins of the Mujahideen and Taliban,
a nation then returned to the Haqqani-Taliban
he'd fled. Now his focus is smaller. More personal,

simpler, reduced. He notices this shift in himself.
Is this it? Is this my friend's new diasporic reality?
Or is it the thinner secular glue that binds us here,

so unlike family, friends and Umma back there.
Is it enough to find joy in small things
happy when the barista doesn't mess up

his morning coffee, and can say his name?
He asks anyone who will listen, *is this a sign*
of mental health problems, should I be worried?

he worries. The world has shifted around him,
chewed him up and spit him out into a new reality,
where medieval thuggee religio-fascists rule

having kicked out the world's super-power,
a reality that diminishes and disempowers him
as with so many other Afghan friends, scattered.

Abraham's Children

She listed epochs and empires,
polities that had grown and shrunk,
holy, from the times before

there were nation states.
Her insistent point was that
they weren't called Palestine.

It was important to her.
So, I ask, why this Palestine
postal stamp? Clearly, here, *Palestine.*

See these photos of a thriving,
multi-ethnic, multi-religious Palestine
in the 30s and 40s, before the *Nakba*?

Muslim, Jewish, Christian, Druze semites
sharing the space of Palestine—they lived, loved,
and said *shabbat shalom salaam* to each other.

They could do again. Peace could bubble
and develop and envelop and protect.
I remember joy *and* surprise when apartheid

ended; the Good Friday when Northern Ireland
built a shaky peace. The impossible can happen!
But I'd lost her. Her mind closed to the possibility

that one day Muslim, Jewish, Christian, & Druze
could share the space of Palestine—to live, love,
and say *shabbat shalom salaam* to each other.

His Ninetieth

Seen through frosted glass darkly
seemed too obvious a last image
for poetry or for memory, but

there it is. He was standing naked,
confused, maybe unsure where he was,
not moving; unnerving, but still,

his outline clear through the bathroom door.
He stayed there too long. I wondered
whether to help, to watch, to stay still—

how to judge between support and intrusion.
The previous day friends, neighbours, family
gathered laughter, celebration, talk, my poem.

This morning is just the two of us—the noise
of young children and ongoing life is elsewhere.
Father, this may be the last image I have of you:

naked, slow, maybe confused, but fearless,
facing up to the world as naked as we all do.
I needed to leave but the dead lock held me still.

JOHN KNOWLES

All Gone

We cleared her house of knickknacks and bric-a-brac.
My brother drove to the dump and calculated worth—
I wanted to know the story of rocks kept in a drawer
But by then I was already too distant to have a say:
Neurodiverse they would now say.
One brother took the burden of care,
One took interest for a roof repaired,
I took a last look at a family home and went back to my own.
And now I look at love letters kept,
Books dusted, polaroid pictures fading—
The small remembrances of a life lived
And wonder
Will anyone understand the draw of rocks
Unlabelled, the loves and dreams
Uncertain, the small boats, French horn,
Clay figures and toys in display cases.
Unlikely that this John Soames-like collection
Will be more than council dump run
For one or other of my sons.

CHRIS ANTHEMUM

Colours

Wearing pink, she places a rose upon the
coffin of her former defender; so the
lines would claim. He died not for nothing, words cry,
draped in the colours.

Red and white and blue are the colours; shrouding
dead and dying soldiers of Empire, shrouding
too the things of love, which were broken, long lost
covenants buried:

Sacrificed and sold for a well of black gold.
Keep the wheels in motion and don't ask why, or
who or where your enemies really are—just
follow the colours.

Father's Day

My father locked himself away,
closed the door and turned the key
for the pleasure of Her Majesty,
day after day after day.

Shame is too liquid to be held by bars.
It flows through locks and taps into glasses.
It runs down throats, along canals, resting in our guts.
There it feeds a yearning, unexpressed.
His compassion was a wild Welsh narcissus,
pressed between the leaves of duty and neglect.

My father locked himself away,
closed the door and turned the key
for the pleasure of Her Majesty,
day after day after day.

One Day the Sun

One day the sun, grown old and corpulent,
will scoff the last of all our fears and hates,
those sour apples past their sell-by dates;
the fiery stomach quenched but discontent.

Then nothing shall remain, not even dreams,
but love will find a space behind the void,
since only nothing can be undestroyed
and zero is the sum of all our schemes,

according to the whisper of the ghost black choir
at two point seven kelvin, radio nought,
one sixty gigahertz FM; where hate and love

are merely eigenstates of one desire,
where true and false are mingled in one thought:
that you, here, now are all it means to live.

ANNY KNIGHT

Maud

On my usual bench, dozing,
staring out at the waves as they chased behind waves,
and the chatter of the pebbles as they shook them all off.
And watching the clouds getting darker around me,
and telling me stories to fill up the day.

I didn't see her arrive or sit down beside me.
No boats today—she said to herself,
Sea's much too rough—I replied.
A shame—she said—but look at the rocks, look at the rocks!

Sitting in silence, with the blue-grey horizon shifting before us,
and the clouds piling up like duvets left out in a doorway,
the clatter of the coastguard helicopter,
getting nearer, getting nearer, circling above us.
I'm Maud—she said—I'm often here.

Then it rained for days on the wind-whipped pebbles,
the beach a restless dream,
the empty promenade a forgotten promise of a better year.
And walking by the beach-huts, holding on to the railings
to stop myself falling,
the bench, too wet to sit on,
but the pale sun catching the worn-out brass plate.
Maud. Lost to the sea.

Doreen is limbo dancing

doreen is limbo dancing between the liminal and literal worlds
blood pressure ridiculously low
oxygen levels disastrous
but her spirits
  can suddenly soar
and we will laugh together as before

Sepsis has not taken her.

but
The x ray revealed she is severely constipated
even though she has constant diarrhoea
A stony shore
Then whooshing tides
her earliest memories were on the potty
and she kept sitting on the bedpan fruitlessly

You do realise you are dying said Dr Fischer
She so reminds me of my own mother
who died at 93 last year
and fought so hard to stay alive.

At home oxygen comes in quick blasts
when I open the window,
no intravenous anything,
but there is medical grade food
grandson made poshnosh of Aldi aubergines and parmesan and

blueberries, bone broth,
birdsong

no 6am reveilles to check you are alive
and insert pharmaceuticals in undignified places.

And no indignant ward mates
accusing me of having a mother
whose snores sound orgasmic.

Your friend, the Robin, flew in

Expelled from the heart ward as a decrepit bed-blocker
Your first wish:
to walk around the garden, smell the roses and see your
    friends the birds.
Try telling an erstwhile Rambler
You'll never walk again
—instead, I said:
We'll work on that.
I thought that we might be able to hoist you up,
plonk you in your chair and do Whacky Races round the garden.
After four attempts the OT team managed to raise you
as though you were a valuable watch in the grabbing machine
                                at the end of the pier.
But then they kept saying:
That hoist must really hurt—doesn't it chafe?
Were they worried about your ticker?
And you sort of agreed
Before we got you into the chair, it was called off
They left looking relieved and acting sympathetic¬.
Eventually the penny dropped:
I think there has been some mistake— I'm not able to get
    out of this bed.
            But at that moment your friend, the robin, flew in.

RICHARD NEWHAM-SULLIVAN
Chosen by Anne Rouse

The Comeback

After years of *bon voyage*, good riddance,
up yours—
fuming and woozy
breath like grease-vents
propping up turnstiles
prong pressing fruit-machines
life hanging by a nudge—

A sea change.

You quit the slots and slobs, and shaved
the streak of losers from your face
with greasy flotsam.
Come wooden panelling.
Come fragrant shops.
Come cherry-cherry-cherry
and a shot at the features board.

Three bright summers.

Three summers you joked less nasty,
talked less doldrums
less yesterday—
less penny horribles
shove-penny, penny piss-ups,
less stain of better times
under each beer mat.

Three bright summers

Like three grapefruit on the win-line
rolled in from nowhere,
from some island
off of Panama,
and cut into segments
left glistening on your table
outside The Gritti.

We dug in, toasting your health.

But then—
nothing terrible.
Little signs. The boot sales on a Sunday.
The old fondness for tat.
That slight smell of grease
returning when you spoke,
and the far-away look
you always had in winter,
staying longer into spring, and then into summer.

Life in the Necropolis

You died on January twentieth.
It was difficult to interpret as death.
You think you would know
but the body is still there.
There are still people and streets and shops.
You still have to eat.
You still have to twist your clothes off at night
and slip quick as a cat into a cold bed.

Only you've died.
And Death is petite, with bird-like bones
dressed in red and smiling, yes,
a quite skullish little grin.
And he's a woman come by as if on a fancy.
And you choose to go with him.

Your husband. Your children. Your home. You watch them
from the window of the van
he calls Princess and wave as they go
without sobbing.
He's interested in your plans. He's softly spoken
and kind. You play word games and share lunch
parked up on the hard shoulder.

But I should have known it was over.
This said with an air of confession
as he splits a roll, offers the bigger half.
Strip-lights in cafés flickered when I passed them,
the needles I kept finding, bad omens.
You kept going for them. He says.
He looks like he's suffered
a thousand deaths already, and another
won't kill him

he listens like the moon in its hood of bone.

Sometimes the Illusion is Ferocious

Having rearranged shadows under a searchlight
the body made its way home
Christmas Eve
labouring under the strain of its luggage
under its secretive despair.
Asking *what will I carry with me?*
And wind was everywhere, everything
the hands clung onto their gifts like amulets
against the storm coming in
the canvas I brought for my brother
pushing against my side like a sail
Wires cracked against concrete
and dark vents spun, where I crawled
along the walls of a backstreet
into the wind's harm
thinking *how many more deaths could I live?*
The antique shops I knew as a child
had taken on the look of the morgue
I could read the paths of the dying
in their amber-lit displays.
And the things I overheard as a child
came back to me in the wind's whisper
when you die you dive back into the ocean
strange to my ear, to thought—but the heart
liked these souls in their luminous life coats
setting off into the dark.
Skinned, at last, the body came
to the corner where it would have to break cover
there were insects instead of graffiti, giant moths
sprayed from dirt, and beyond
the monomaniacal waves.
I stood like a thief in the darkness,
asking *how could I go on?*
Past the church, where they buried him
to her flat, giddy with grief,
weighed down with my gifts and the canvas
weighed down by my thoughts
seagulls losing their pivot

losing the battle against their own wings.
But the body kept refusing its bondage
I would arrive—
I would close all the shutters
on the dark hum of the tide,
and if they rattled, it was not a death rattle
and we would talk and she would make tea
and we would listen to Leonard Cohen
and it would be Christmas Eve.

Out of Everywhere

But then one day—a tipping point.
A twin's born of this pebble beach
but where you might just step into the breach
of a simple stone and walk in its crystal cove.

Today content with *what you must*,
three moments a week to watch your fitful breath,
and up to the neck (again) in buried grief
for the sake of who knows what—

but free—still free to burn dry wood
and curl up late, as homeless as the tide,
the shifting rush of speech as waves pull back;
the sea says shush, and look, the stones don't speak.

BILL WYATT

Haiku

Stopping off
In nirvana—I nearly missed
The last bus home

Don't have the heart
To brush away the cobweb—
Let the wind do it

Beneath the lamp
Sweeping up moths—offering
Them to Buddha

Neither for the world
Nor against it—daffodil
Swaying in the breeze

Ashtray

That
ashtray
chipped

is only
mind's
indifference

to love,
or else
a reminder

of
ourselves
as an

ashtray
would
have us

Street Bodhisattvas, *a haibun*

I am on my way to the bottle bank
doing my bit for the environment.
Passing the Big Issue seller & his dog,
I don't have any change & make a note to
catch him on the way out of Somerfields.
Approaching the corner, a young girl
is screaming at her kid.
"Namu Kanzeon Bosatsu." She looks as though
just out of school. The kid can only
be a couple of years before he starts school.
He's bawling & she's screaming at him to be quiet.
Everyone turning around & looking at them.
Suddenly, out of nowhere, a fellow appears,
hollering & shouting at the girl, they are head to head.
"how do you like being screamed at" he yells.
She starts right back at him, hurling abuse.
"Namu Kanzeon Bosatsu." Everyone stops in their tracks.
He's red faced, on a cider high.
I step in, calmly holding him back
Saying "Keep cool".
Anger a fire in the heart
That burns up a forest of merit.
He looks at me, with that sad weariness
of years of ill treatment.
We connect, & after a few brief words
he continues on his way,
saying "Thanks mate, you're a gentleman".
I empty my bottles, musing
that we are all on the way to enlightenment -
the vendor and his dog,
The screaming girl & kid, the cider addict
& the bystanders.
All of us potential Bodhisattvas

*

Just a cloud chaser
that's me—in the midst of it all
a bright shining pearl

HENRY NORMAL

The Difference Engine

The first computers were human

then machines were made to add
and subtract

These machines then multiplied
and divided

inspired by revolution and
The mathematics of the stars
difference became analytical

Helped by the daughter of a poet
And Jacquard's loom

Helped by war, the vacuum
and the hydrogen bomb

On and off
zero and one

Different people
made a difference

to make Turing complete

Winchelsea Beach in Winter

In perfect step our footprints disappear
as soon as we raise each shoe

The beach resembles an ice rink
^m e l t i n g

Our reflections
    keep us in balance

The   sky   is   so   wide   it
tints and tilts the sea, the clouds and even the sand

        Cliff end
has a quiff

Seagulls dot the scene
Like flecks on a lens

The horizon enters our ears
Hands are tucked into sleeves

You might consider our shapes odd
finding their own angle on this earth

You could be forgiven for thinking
we are walking on water

Sit Down Poetry

Like Shakespeare
but on a chair
Like John Keats
but on seats
Like Elizabeth Barrett Brown
but sitting down
Like Seigfred Sassoon
but sitting doon

Like William Blake
but taking a break
Like Ted Hughes
with no legs used
Like Peter Porter
only shorter
Like Simon Armitage
but more Simon Armchair-age

Like Wordsworth
but nearer the earth
Like Ezra Pound
but nearer the ground
Like Walt Whitman
but having a sit, man

Like T.S. Eliot
if his feet were delicate
Like Rudyard Kipling
if his shoes were crippling
Like Roger McGough
with his legs sawn off
Like Edith Sitwell
sitting well

Like Aristophanes
with dodgy knees
Like D.H. Lawrence
with a standing abhorrence

Like Charles Baudelaire
assis sur le derrière

Like Edgar Allen Poe
if he'd stubbed his toe
Like Percy Bysshe Shelley
if his legs were jelly
Like Longfellow
but shorter

Like the Brontë sisters
with painful blisters
Like Luke Wright
but half his height
Like ee cummings
but more shortcomings

Like Maya Angelou
if she'd lost a shoe
Like Robert Frost
if both shoes were lost
Like Benjamin Zephania
but Zephan-lower

Like Philip Larkin
but not racist

The Fire Hills

Sunset in mid-December
the skyline lit like dying embers

Pitch as the
immediate landscape appears
the distance
promises a new dawn
somewhere on our shared Earth

High tide at our hind
night closing in
We raise our eyes to the fading glow
climb the slope
And haul our cold bones home

Better Days

Midwinter we yearn for spring
Midnight we look to the dawn
We hope for better days

We make plans for when we are stronger
when infection has passed
when the fracture has healed

We ready ourselves for the longest of roads
We study to stand in good stead
We strive so at some stage we can rest

Yet even on the sunniest days
we prepare for the coming storm

We bide our time
We watch our step
We correct our course

We pray for someone
or something
to take us somewhere

somewhere better

We spend our whole lives
searching for better days
and when we look back
there they were

We are the someone we prayed for
We are the something
This is the somewhere better

These are the better days
These are the better days

Oli Spleen on the High Street, Old Town

CLASSIC POEMS

INTRODUCTION TO CLASSIC POEMS

Hastings is a place of muses.

They're like the tides and winds: invisible forces only known by their effects.

In ancient mythology, the muses were nine goddesses who protected the sciences and arts. Later, one or two of the punkier deities must have got lost on their windy travels and shored up on the Sussex coast. For centuries since, they have been going around town doing mischief: rustling Alan Turing's papers and the tassels on Grey Owl's moccasins. Blowing a gale up Robert Tressell's ragged trousers. Loitering to whisper in John Logie Baird's shell-like. Or just flying over the troublesome waves, flicking salty spirals from their lovely locks.

To locals of the Bo Peep Pub in West St. Leonards, it may come as a surprise that one of the greatest English poets drank with his muse there (or thereabouts) two centuries ago, the intelligent, enigmatic and beautiful Isabella Jones. Bo Peep, today's St Leonards-On-Sea, was something of a hotspot for sheep-thieving smugglers – hence the nursery rhyme. But for John Keats, it was where he worked on his poem *Endymion* – and on Isabella too; an older woman, who inspired an upthrust of creativity in the young poet. It was she who suggested the topic for a number of Keats's poems and was the subject of several others, such as *Hush! Hush! Tread Softly!* and *You Say You Love.*[1]

While it is historically accurate that Christina Rossetti first came to Hastings for the health benefits, *her* muse, in the form of cerebral odd-pot poet Charles Bagot Cayley, was ready to meet her here. Cayley was a former student of her father at King's College, London, but his family home was on Pevensey Road in St Leonards. Immortalized as the "dearest Friend" and erstwhile love of Rossetti, Cayley's impact on her is captured most beautifully in her sequence, *Monna Innominata: A Sonnet of Sonnets*, where she writes:

> *Thinking of you, and all that was, and all*
> *That might have been and now can never be,*
> *I feel your honour'd excellence, and see*
> *Myself unworthy of the happier call.*[2]

In 1866, Cayley proposed, but Rossetti refused due to their religious differences, believing that to marry him was to betray her faith. However, they remained close, and even after his death Cayley continued to be a living personality in her heart according to Rossetti's brother, William.[3] In 1884, a year after his death, Rossetti visited Cayley's grave in Hastings Cemetery, writing the moving elegy, 'One Sea-Side Grave' about her visit.

Hastings itself was something of a muse for Christina Rossetti too. In 'The Waves of This Troublesome World: A Tale of Hastings Ten Years Ago', she writes: "Perhaps there is no pleasanter watering-place in England where to spend the fine summer months than Hastings, on the Sussex coast."

In the early part of that story, she captures the atmosphere of the place: "The old town, nestling in a long, narrow valley, flanked by the East and West Hills, looks down upon the sea. At the valley mouth, on the shingly beach, stands the fish-market, where boatmen disembark the fruit of daily toil... It is a pretty sight in brilliant holiday weather to watch the many parties of health or pleasure-seekers which throng the beach. Boys and girls picking up shells, pebbles, and star-fishes, or raising with hands and wooden spades a sand fortress, encircled by a moat full of sea-water, and crowned by a twig of seaweed as a flag."[4]

Another depiction in this era (or just before) comes from Thomas Hood's poem, 'A Storm at Hastings, or The Little Unknown'.[5] Hood honeymooned in the town, and while his new wife was admiring the handsome sailors, the poet and humorist soaked up an atmosphere which would permeate his comic and somewhat eerie narrative poem. The Hastings he describes is strangely familiar. It's full of "crowds of idlers" and coachfuls of city tourists trying their luck in the arcades, bracing themselves for the chilly sea or looking for a seaside fling. In the poem, a curious man with infuriatingly good luck brings controversy one Friday by winning everything in sight, horrifying the other visitors. That is, until an epic storm puts him firmly in his place.

In a letter from the time, Hood also tells of taking a trip to Church in the Wood near Hollington, the place so admired by essayist Charles Lamb. "There it stands, like the first idea of a Church, before parishioners were thought of, nothing but birds for its congregation,"[6] Lamb wrote. Hood is rather sardonic about Lamb's romantic use of language to describe the church though: only showing that one man's muse is another's mockery.[7]

The Hastings Muses are not always in a charming mood, as is obvious from 'The Homeless Ghost' by George MacDonald. In that narrative poem, a spooky late-night walk from a seaside pub leads to a strange proposition from a ghost of sublime and chilling beauty. The sea view from MacDonald's residence at the foot of the East Hill is captured dramatically:

> Till a gust of wind against the pane,
> Mixed with a sea-bird's cries,
> And the sudden spatter of drifting rain
> Bade him mark the altered skies.
>
> The moon was gone, entombed in cloud;
> The wind began to rave;
> The ocean heaved within its shroud,
> For the dark had built its grave

MacDonald was a poet and author of formidable talent—known as the 'grandfather of fantasy', he was admired by C.S. Lewis among others, who wrote, "I have never concealed the fact that I regarded George MacDonald as my master".[8]

He was a mentor of Lewis Carroll too, who also visited Hastings regularly while a student, staying with his aunt in Wellington Square.[9] It was MacDonald, in fact, who encouraged Carroll to send *Alice in Wonderland* for publication.

MacDonald completed his famous novel *Phantastes* while residing in the town. He stayed in several locations, and there is a blue plaque in his honour where he lived on Tackleway, just up the road from the former home of another notable historical figure, Lady Isabella Noel Byron.[10]

Lady Byron (aka Anne Isabella Milbanke) was many things, including a pioneer of the Co-operative movement—an original member of the institute in George Street in the Old Town. However, she remains most widely known for being the former wife of the poet Lord Byron (who also visited the Hastings on occasion) and mother of Ada Lovelace, the genius mathematician. Having allegedly discovered that Byron was up to no good with his half-sister, Lady Byron broke off their marriage after just one year— much to Byron's chagrin as can be seen in his poem 'Fare Thee Well'. In later life, Lady Byron became the patron for George MacDonald, and it was she who recommended he move to Hastings for respite following a health condition.[11]

George MacDonald and Lewis Carroll were on friendly terms with another poet residing locally, Coventry Patmore. Patmore lived in Hastings from 1875–1891. He can be linked to a number of historical buildings in the area: Old Hastings House, where he lived. St Mary Star of the Sea, which he helped fund to build. And the Convent of the Holy Child, where his daughter Emily Honoria was ordained.[12] A very

Victorian Victorian poet, Patmore later became the target of Virginia Woolf's critical razor-blade. It was his antiquated views of women as self-sacrificing and child-like in *The Angel in the House*, which rightly got Woolf's goat. In an essay on the topic, Woolf, in no uncertain terms, called for the angel to be done away with.[13] Some of Patmore's lyric poems have, however, survived the test of time, particularly 'Magna Est Veritas' which gives us a view into his solitary, reflective walks, possibly at Rock-a-Nore:

> *Here, in this little Bay,*
> *Full of tumultuous life and great repose,*
> *Where, twice a day,*
> *The purposeless, glad ocean comes and goes,*
> *Under high cliffs, and far from the huge town,*
> *I sit me down.*

There can be few muses as tragic and ethereal as Elizabeth Siddal—a gifted artist whose work has been exhibited internationally, as well as a poet and artist's model for the Pre-Raphaelite artists. "Magnificently tall, with a lovely figure... she has grey eyes, and her hair is like dazzling copper."[14] That's how Walter Deverell described Siddal, who he introduced to the Pre-Raphaelite brotherhood, a group of renowned painters fascinated with medieval revivalism of the Italianate variety. For a decade, she would be their inspiration, personifying their ideal of beauty. She was perhaps most famously depicted as Ophelia lying among the reeds by John Everett Millais (Millais actually having her lie in a bathtub while he painted – adding to the realism – and giving her pneumonia). She stayed in Hastings often, and moved to the Old Town in 1860, marrying painter and poet Dante Gabriel Rossetti at St. Clements Church in the old town the same year.[15]

Dante Gabriel Rossetti's obsession for Siddal is both exhilarating and horrifying. His paintings and drawings of her number into their thousands. Dante himself writes of her image seeming to be alive to him in 'The Portrait', and his sister Christina also describes his mounting obsession in her poem, 'In an Artist's Studio': "He feeds upon her face day and night." Siddal died of a laudanum overdose, which was likely to have been suicide, only two years after their marriage. Dante Rossetti was so distraught at her passing that he chose to bury his poems alongside her. However, some time later, persuaded by friends, he decided to exhume the body to retrieve them for publication.

Of all the themes connected to Hastings which have inspired writers, the most famous is, of course, the battle of 1066. Marriott Edgar's 'The Battle of Hastings' is perhaps one of the most enduring and well-loved for its funny slant, where William and Harold opt for a game of football to resolve their differences. The poet Stephen Phillips wrote a more sombre account in his verse play *Harold*.[16] Phillips retired to the town in 1909, living at 13 Wellington Road and later on Brook Street. Phillips was for a while a very famous poet and playwright—his version of *Ulysses* being performed before royalty. His poem, 'By The Sea', shares an intimate and transcendent moment between young lovers after a walk along the coastal path.

It was just over one hundred years ago that the author and Hastings-resident Coulson Kernahan wrote a book in which he said: "Hastings and St. Leonards are justly proud of the celebrities who have either lived or, for a time, made their home in the neighbourhood."[17] The celebrities referred to included many of these poets and authors, whose stories were once wrapped up with the town's identity. Back then, it was taken for granted that the town's connection with the 'world of letters', as it was called, was as much a part of its nature as the salty sea air and shingly beach. Even the town's MP was once a well-known poet called Edmund

Waller. But somewhere along the way this celebration of the power of the written word in Hastings became buried. The story the town told itself became more mundane. The history of classic poets and writers, their tales and rhymes, their muses and obsessions, was lost.

One hundred years on, a great deal more has happened to tie Hastings to the 'world of letters'. But where is the fanfare? Where is the celebration? It is left to local festivals and not-for-profit newspapers to raise the flag, while elsewhere, it is too often ignored. The hope is, with the publication of this book comes a re-imagining of our town for locals and visitors alike, as a place that is as alive today as it's ever been with poetry and stories worth relishing.

Notes

1. Thomson H. Fanny Brawne and Other Women. In: O'Neill M, ed. John Keats in Context. Literature in Context. Cambridge University Press; 2017:38-46.

2. Rossetti, Christina. "Monna Innominata: A Sonnet of Sonnets." A Pageant and Other Poems, London: Macmillan, 1881.

3. Rossetti, William Michael. Reminiscences of Charles Bagot Cayley. In The Family Letters of Christina Rossetti. Edited by William Michael Rossetti. London: Macmillan, 1908.

4. Rossetti, Christina. "The Waves of this Troublesome World: A Tale of Hastings Ten Years Ago." The Churchman's Shilling Magazine, April and May 1867. Later published in Commonplace and Other Stories, London: F.S. Ellis, 1870.

5. Hood, Thomas. Poems of Thomas Hood. London: Ward, Lock and Co., 1883.

6. Lamb, Charles. "A Quaker's Meeting." The Works of Charles and Mary Lamb. Edited by E. V. Lucas, London: Methuen & Co., 1903, pp. 191-192.

7. Hood, Thomas. "The Letters of Thomas Hood." Edited by Peter F. Morgan, Toronto: University of Toronto Press,1973.

8. Quoted in George MacDonald, The Complete Fairy Tales (Penguin Classics, 2000)

9. Collingwood, Stuart Dodgson. The Life and Letters of Lewis Carroll. New York: The Century Co., 1899, p. 81.

10. Raeper, William. George MacDonald. Tring, Herts: Lion Publishing, 1987, p. 142.

11. Mayne, Ethel Colburn. The Life and Letters of Anne Isabella, Lady Noel Byron: From Unpublished Papers in the Possession of the Late Ralph, Earl of Lovelace. New York: C. Scribner's, 1929, p. 390.

12. Champneys, Basil. Memoirs and Correspondence of Coventry Patmore. London: George Bell & Sons, 1900.

13. Woolf, Virginia. "Professions for Women." The Death of the Moth and Other Essays, London: Hogarth Press, 1942.

14. Hunt, William Holman. "Pre-Raphaelitism and the Pre-Raphaelite Brotherhood." Vol. I, London: Macmillan, 1905.

15. Rossetti, Gabriele Dante. The Letters of Gabriele Dante Rossetti. Edited by William Michael Rossetti, London: Ellis and Elvey, 1897.

16. Phillips, Stephen. Harold - A Chronicle Play. London: John Lane, 1927.

17. Kernahan, Coulson. Celebrities: Little Stories About Famous Folk, London: Hutchinson & Co, 1923, p. 214-215.

A Smuggler's Song

If you wake at midnight, and hear a horse's feet,
Don't go drawing back the blind, or looking in the street,
Them that ask no questions isn't told a lie.
Watch the wall, my darling, while the Gentlemen go by!
    Five and twenty ponies,
    Trotting through the dark—
    Brandy for the Parson,
    Baccy for the Clerk.
    Laces for a lady; letters for a spy,
And watch the wall, my darling, while the Gentlemen go by!

Running round the woodlump if you chance to find
Little barrels, roped and tarred, all full of brandy-wine,
Don't you shout to come and look, nor use 'em for your play.
Put the brishwood back again—and they'll be gone next day!

If you see the stable-door setting open wide;
If you see a tired horse lying down inside;
If your mother mends a coat cut about and tore;
If the lining's wet and warm—don't you ask no more!

If you meet King George's men, dressed in blue and red,
You be careful what you say, and mindful what is said.
If they call you "pretty maid," and chuck you 'neath the chin,
Don't you tell where no one is, nor yet where no one's been!

Knocks and footsteps round the house—whistles after dark—
You've no call for running out till the house-dogs bark.
Trusty's here, and Pincher's here, and see how dumb they lie—
They don't fret to follow when the Gentlemen go by!

If you do as you've been told, 'likely there's a chance,
You'll be give a dainty doll, all the way from France,
With a cap of Valenciennes, and a velvet hood—
A present from the Gentlemen, along 'o being good!

Five and twenty ponies
Trotting through the dark—
Brandy for the Parson,
Baccy for the Clerk.
Them that asks no questions isn't told a lie—
Watch the wall, my darling, while the Gentlemen go by!

By the Sea

Remember, ah remember, how we walked
Together on the sea-cliff! You were come
From bathing in the ocean and the sea
Was not yet dry upon your hair: together
We walked in the wet wind till we were far
From voices, even from the thoughts of men.
Remember how on the warm beach we sat
By the old barque, and in the smell of tar;
While the full ocean on the pebbles dropped,
And in our ears the intimate low wind
Of noon, that breathing from some ancient place,
Blew on us merely sleep and pungent youth.
So deeply glad we grew that in pure joy
Closer we came; your wild and wet dark hair
Slashed in my eyes your essence and your sting.
We had no thought; we troubled not to speak;
Slowly your head fell down upon my breast,
In the soft breeze the acquiescing sun;
And the sea-bloom, the colour of calm wind,
Was on your cheek; like children then we kissed,
Innocent with the sea and pure with air;
My spirit fled into thee. The moon climbed,
The sea formed nearer, and we two arose;
But ah, how tranquil from that deep embrace!
And with no sadness from that natural kiss:
Beautiful indolence was on our brains,
And on our limbs as we together swayed
Between the luminous ocean and dark fields.
We two in vivid slumber without haste,
Returned; while veil on veil the heaven was bared;
And a new glory was on land and sea,
And the moist evening fallow, richly dark
Sent up to us the odour cold of sleep,
The infinite sweet of death: so we returned,
Delaying ever, calm companions,
Peacefully slow beside the moody heave
Of the moon-brilliant billow to the town.

CHRISTINA ROSSETTI

from Monna Innominata: Sonnet of Sonnets

1.

Come back to me, who wait and watch for you—
Or come not yet, for it is over then,
And long it is before you come again,
So far between my pleasures are and few.
While, when you come not, what I do I do
Thinking "Now when he comes, my sweetest when:"
For one man is my world of all the men
This wide world holds; O love, my world is you.
Howbeit, to meet you grows almost a pang
Because the pang of parting comes so soon;
My hope hangs waning, waxing, like a moon
Between the heavenly days on which we meet:
Ah me, but where are now the songs I sang
When life was sweet because you called them sweet?

2.

I wish I could remember that first day,
First hour, first moment of your meeting me,
If bright or dim the season, it might be
Summer or winter for aught I can say;
So unrecorded did it slip away,
So blind was I to see and to foresee,
So dull to mark the budding of my tree
That would not blossom yet for many a May.
If only I could recollect it, such
A day of days! I let it come and go
As traceless as a thaw of bygone snow;
It seemed to mean so little, meant so much;
If only now I could recall that touch,
First touch of hand in hand—Did one but know!

In an Artist's Studio

One face looks out from all his canvases,
One selfsame figure sits or walks or leans:
We found her hidden just behind those screens,
That mirror gave back all her loveliness.
A queen in opal or in ruby dress,
A nameless girl in freshest summer-greens,
A saint, an angel—every canvas means
The same one meaning, neither more or less.
He feeds upon her face by day and night,
And she with true kind eyes looks back on him,
Fair as the moon and joyful as the light:
Not wan with waiting, not with sorrow dim;
Not as she is, but was when hope shone bright;
Not as she is, but as she fills his dream.

By the Sea

Why does the sea moan evermore?
Shut out from heaven it makes its moan,
It frets against the boundary shore;
All earth's full rivers cannot fill
The sea, that drinking thirsteth still.

Sheer miracles of loveliness
Lie hid in its unlooked-on bed:
Anemones, salt, passionless,
Blow flower-like; just enough alive
To blow and multiply and thrive.

Shells quaint with curve, or spot, or spike,
Encrusted live things argus-eyed,
All fair alike, yet all unlike,
Are born without a pang, and die
Without a pang, and so pass by.

One Sea-Side Grave

Unmindful of the roses,
Unmindful of the thorn,
A reaper tired reposes
Among his gathered corn:
So might I, till the morn!

Cold as the cold Decembers,
Past as the days that set,
While only one remembers
And all the rest forget—
But one remembers yet.

A Dirge

Why were you born when the snow was falling?
You should have come to the cuckoo's calling,
Or when grapes are green in the cluster,
Or, at least, when lithe swallows muster
For their far off flying
From summer dying.

Why did you die when the lambs were cropping?
You should have died at the apples' dropping,
When the grasshopper comes to trouble,
And the wheat-fields are sodden stubble,
And all winds go sighing
For sweet things dying.

Remember

Remember me when I am gone away,
Gone far away into the silent land;
When you can no more hold me by the hand,
Nor I half turn to go yet turning stay.
Remember me when no more day by day
You tell me of our future that you planned:
Only remember me; you understand
It will be late to counsel then or pray.
Yet if you should forget me for a while
And afterwards remember, do not grieve:
For if the darkness and corruption leave
A vestige of the thoughts that once I had,
Better by far you should forget and smile
Than that you should remember and be sad.

JOHN KEATS

Hush, Hush! Tread Softly!

1.

Hush, hush! tread softly! hush, hush my dear!
All the house is asleep, but we know very well
That the jealous, the jealous old bald-pate may hear.
Though you've padded his night-cap—O sweet Isabel!
Though your feet are more light than a Fairy's feet,
Who dances on bubbles where brooklets meet—
Hush, hush! soft tiptoe! hush, hush my dear!
For less than a nothing the jealous can hear.

2.

No leaf doth tremble, no ripple is there
On the river—all's still, and the night's sleepy eye
Closes up, and forgets all its Lethean care,
Charmed to death by the drone of the humming May-fly;
And the Moon, whether prudish or complaisant,
Hath fled to her bower, well knowing I want
No light in the dusk, no torch in the gloom,
But my Isabel's eyes, and her lips pulped with bloom.

3.

Lift the latch! ah gently! ah tenderly – sweet!
We are dead if that latchet gives one little chink!
Well done—now those lips, and a flowery seat—
The old man may sleep, and the planets may wink;
The shut rose shall dream of our loves, and awake
Full blown, and such warmth for the morning's take;
The stock-dove shall hatch her soft brace and shall coo,
While I kiss to the melody, aching all through!

Lines

Unfelt, unheard, unseen,
I've left my little queen,
Her languid arms in silver slumber lying:
Ah! through their nestling touch,
Who—who could tell how much
There is for madness—cruel, or complying?

Those faery lids how sleek!
Those lips how moist—they speak,
In ripest quiet, shadows of sweet sounds:
Into my fancy's ear,
Melting a burden dear,
How 'Love doth know no fullness nor no bounds.'

True!—tender memoirs!
I bend upon your laws:
This sweetest day for dalliance was born!
So, without more ado,
I'll feel my heaven anew,
For all the blushing of the hasty morn.

You Say You Love

1.

You say you love; but with a voice
Chaster than a nun's, who singeth
The soft Vespers to herself
While the chime-bell ringeth—
O love me truly!

2.

You say you love; but with a smile
Cold as sunrise in September,
As you were Saint Cupid's nun,
And kept his weeks of Ember.
O love me truly!

3.

You say you love but then your lips
Coral tinted teach no blisses,
More than coral in the sea
They never pout for kisses
O love me truly!

4.

You say you love; but then your hand
No soft squeeze for squeeze returneth,
It is like a statue's dead
While mine to passion burneth
O love me truly!

5.

O breathe a word or two of fire!
Smile, as if those words should burn me,
Squeeze as lovers should O kiss
And in thy heart inurn me!
O love me truly!

from Isabella; or, The Pot of Basil

With every morn their love grew tenderer,
With every eve deeper and tenderer still;
He might not in house, field or garden stir,
But her full shape would all his seeing fill;
And his continual voice was pleasanter
To her than noise of trees of hidden rill;
Her lute-string give an echo of his name,
She spoilt her half-done broidery with the same.

DANTE GABRIEL ROSSETTI

Sudden Light

I have been here before,
But when or how I cannot tell:
I know the grass beyond the door,
The sweet keen smell,
The sighing sound, the lights around the shore.

You have been mine before—
How long ago I may not know:
But just when at that swallow's soar
Your neck turned so,
Some veil did fall—I knew it all of yore.

Has this been thus before?
And shall not thus time's eddying flight
Still with our lives our love restore
In death's despite,
And day and night yield one delight once more?

Insomnia

Thin are the night-skirts left behind
By daybreak hours that onward creep,
And thin, alas! the shred of sleep
That wavers with the spirit's wind:
But in half-dreams that shift and roll
And still remember and forget,
My soul this hour has drawn your soul
A little nearer yet.

Our lives, most dear, are never near,
Our thoughts are never far apart,
Though all that draws us heart to heart
Seems fainter now and now more clear.
To-night Love claims his full control,
And with desire and with regret
My soul this hour has drawn your soul
A little nearer yet.

Is there a home where heavy earth
Melts to bright air that breathes no pain,
Where water leaves no thirst again
And springing fire is Love's new birth?
If faith long bound to one true goal
May there at length its hope beget,
My soul that hour shall draw your soul
For ever nearer yet.

Even So

So it is, my dear.
All such things touch secret strings
For heavy hearts to hear.
So it is, my dear.

Very like indeed:
Sea and sky, afar, on high,
Sand and strewn seaweed—
Very like indeed.

But the sea stands spread
As one wall with the flat skies,
Where the lean black craft like flies
Seem well-nigh stagnated,
Soon to drop off dead.

Seemed it so to us
When I was thine and thou wast mine,
And all these things were thus,
But all our world in us?

Could we be so now?
Not if all beneath heaven's pall
Lay dead but I and thou,
Could we be so now!

from The Portrait

This is her picture as she was:
It seems a thing to wonder on,
As though mine image in the glass
Should tarry when myself am gone.
I gaze until she seems to stir—
Until mine eyes almost aver
That now, even now, the sweet lips part
To breathe the words of the sweet heart—
And yet the earth is over her.

ELIZABETH SIDDAL

Worn Out

Thy strong arms are around me, love
My head is on thy breast;
Low words of comfort come from thee
Yet my soul has no rest.

For I am but a startled thing
Nor can I ever be
Aught save a bird whose broken wing
Must fly away from thee.

I cannot give to thee the love
I gave so long ago,
The love that turned and struck me down
Amid the blinding snow.

I can but give a failing heart
And weary eyes of pain,
A faded mouth that cannot smile
And may not laugh again.

Yet keep thine arms around me, love,
Until I fall to sleep;
Then leave me, saying no goodbye
Lest I might wake, and weep.

Gone

To touch the glove upon her tender hand,
To watch the jewel sparkle in her ring,
Lifted my heart into a sudden song
As when the wild birds sing.

To touch her shadow on the sunny grass,
To break her pathway through the darkened wood,
Filled all my life with trembling and tears
And silence where I stood.

I watch the shadows gather round my heart,
I live to know that she is gone—
Gone gone for ever, like the tender dove
That left the Ark alone.

THOMAS HOOD

from A Storm At Hastings, And The Little Unknown

'Twas August—Hastings every day was filling—
Hastings, that "greenest spot on memory's waste"!
With crowds of idlers willing and unwilling
To be bedipped—be noticed—or be braced,
And all things rose a penny in a shilling.
Meanwhile, from window, and from door, in haste
"Accommodation bills" kept coming down,
Gladding "the world of-letters" in that town.

Each day poured in new coachfuls of new cits,
Flying from London smoke and dust annoying,
Unmarried Misses hoping to make hits,
And new-wed couples fresh from Tunbridge toying,
Lacemen and placemen, ministers and wits,
And Quakers of both sexes, much enjoying
A morning's reading by the ocean's rim,
That sect delighting in the sea's broad brim.

And lo! amongst all these appeared a creature,
So small, he almost might a twin have been
With Miss Crachami - dwarfish quite in stature,
Yet well proportioned - neither fat nor lean,
His face of marvellously pleasant feature,
So short and sweet a man was never seen—
All thought him charming at the first beginning—
Alas, ere long they found him far too winning!

He seemed in love with chance—and chance repaid
His ardent passion with her fondest smile,
The sunshine of good luck, without a shade,
He staked and won—and won and staked—the bile
It stirred of many a man and many a maid,
To see at every venture how that vile
Small gambler snatched—and how he won them too—
A living Pam, omnipotent at loo!

Miss Wiggins set her heart upon a box,
'Twas handsome rosewood, and inlaid with brass,
And dreamt three times she garnished it with stocks
Of needles, silks, and cottons—but, alas!
She lost it wide awake. We thought Miss Cox
Was lucky—but she saw three caddies pass
To that small imp; no living luck could loo him!
Sir Stamford would have lost his Raffles to him!

And so he climbed—and rode—and won—and walked,
The wondrous topic of the curious swarm
That haunted the Parade. Many were balked
Of notoriety by that small form
Pacing it up and down: some even talked
Of ducking him—when lo! a dismal storm
Stopped in—one Friday, at the close of day—
And every head was turned another way—

Watching the grander guest. It seemed to rise
Bulky and slow upon the southern brink
Of the horizon—fanned by sultry sighs—
So black and threatening, I cannot think
Of any simile, except the skies
Miss Wiggins sometimes shades in Indian ink—
Mis-shapen blotches of such heavy vapour,
They seem a deal more solid than her paper.

As for the sea, it did not fret, and rave,
And tear its waves to tatters, and so dash on
The stony-hearted beach; some bards would have
It always rampant, in that idle fashion—
Whereas the waves rolled in, subdued and grave,
Like schoolboys, when the master's in a passion,
Who meekly settle in and take their places,
With a very quiet awe on all their faces.

* * *

So fierce the lightning flashed. In all their days
The oldest smugglers had not seen such flashing,
And they are used to many a pretty blaze,
To keep their Hollands from an awkward clashing
With hostile cutters in our creeks and bays:
And truly one could think, without much lashing
The fancy, that those coasting clouds, so awful
And black, were fraught with spirits as unlawful.

The gay Parade grew thin—all the fair crowd
Vanished—as if they knew their own attractions—
For now the lightning through a near-hand cloud
Began to make some very crooked fractions—
Only some few remained that were not cowed,
A few rough sailors, who had been in actions,
And sundry boatmen, that with quick yeos,
Lest it should blow—were pulling up the Rose:

(No flower, but a boat)—some more were hauling
The Regent by the head: another crew
With that same cry peculiar to their calling—
Were heaving up the Hope: and as they knew
The very gods themselves oft get a mauling
In their own realms, the seamen wisely drew
The Neptune rather higher on the beach,
That he might lie beyond his billows' reach.

And now the storm, with its despotic power,
Had all usurped the azure of the skies,
Making our daylight darker by an hour,
And some few drops—of an unusual size—
Few and distinct—scarce twenty to the shower,
Fell like huge teardrops from a giant's eyes—
But then this sprinkle thickened in a trice
And rained much harder—in good solid ice.

***

As parcel of the cloud—the clouds themselves,
Like monstrous crags and summits everlasting,
Piled each on each in most gigantic shelves,
That Milton's devils were engaged in blasting.
We could e'en fancy Satan and his elves
Busy upon those crags, and ever casting
Huge fragments loose—and that we felt the sound
They made in falling to the startled ground.

And so the tempest scowled away—and soon
Timidly shining through its skirts of jet,
We saw the rim of the pacific moon,
Like a bright fish entangled in a net,
Flashing its silver sides—how sweet a boon
Seemed her sweet light, as though it would beget,
With that fair smile, a calm upon the seas—
Peace in the sky—and coolness in the breeze!

Meantime the hail had ceased—and all the brood
Of glaziers stole abroad to count their gains;
At every window there were maids who stood
Lamenting o'er the glass's small remains,
Or with coarse linens made the fractions good,
Stanching the wind in all the wounded panes—
Or, holding candles to the panes, in doubt
The wind resolved blowing the candles out.

No house was whole that had a southern front—
No greenhouse but the same mishap befell;
Bow-windows and bell-glasses bore the brunt—
No sex in glass was spared! For those who dwell
On each hill-side, you might have swum a punt
In any of their parlors; Mrs. Snell
Was slopped out of her seat,—and Mr. Hitchin
Had a flower-garden washed into a Kitchen.

But still the sea was mild, and quite disclaimed
The recent violence. Each after each
The gentle waves a gentle murmur framed,
Tapping, like woodpeckers, the hollow beach.
Howbeit his weather eye the seaman aimed
Across the calm, and hinted by his speech
A gale next morning—and when morning broke,
There was a gale—"quite equal to bespoke."

Before high water—(it were better far
To christen it not water then, but waiter,
For then the tide is serving at the bar)
Rose such a swell—I never saw one greater!
Black, jagged billows rearing up in war
Like ragged roaring bears against the baiter,
With lots of froth upon the shingle shed,
Like stout poured out with a fine beachy head.

No open boat was open to a fare,
Or launched that morn on seven-shilling trips;
No bathing woman waded—none would dare
A dipping in the wave—but waived their dips;
No seagull ventured on the stormy air,
And all the dreary coast was clear of ships;
For two lea shores upon the River Lea
Are not so perilous as one at sea.

Awe-struck we sat, and gazed upon the scene
Before us in such horrid hurly-burly—
A boiling ocean of mixed black and green,
A sky of copper color, grim and surly—
When lo, in that vast hollow scooped between
Two rolling Alps of water—white and curly!
We saw a pair of little arms a-skimming,
Much like a first or last attempt at swimming!

Sometimes a hand—sometimes a little shoe—
Sometime a skirt—sometimes a hank of hair
Just like a dabbled seaweed rose to view,
Sometimes a knee—sometimes a back was bare—
At last a frightful summerset he threw
Right on the shingles. Any one could swear
The lad was dead—without a chance of perjury,
And battered by the surge beyond all surgery!

However, we snatched up the corse thus thrown,
Intending, Christian-like, to sod and turf it,
And after venting Pity's sigh and groan,
Then curiosity began with her fit;
And lo! the features of the Small Unknown!
'Twas he that of the surf had had this surfeit!
And in his fob, the cause of late monopolies,
We found a contract signed with Mephistopheles!

A bond of blood, whereby the sinner gave
His forfeit soul to Satan in reversion,
Providing in this world he was to have
A lordship over luck, by whose exertion
He might control the course of cards and brave
All throws of dice—but on a sea excursion
The juggling demon, in his usual vein,
Seized the last cast—and Nicked him in the main!

COVENTRY PATMORE

Magna Est Veritas

  Here, in this little Bay,
Full of tumultuous life and great repose,
Where, twice a day,
The purposeless, glad ocean comes and goes,
Under high cliffs, and far from the huge town,
I sit me down.
For want of me the world's course will not fail:
When all its work is done, the lie shall rot;
The truth is great, and shall prevail,
When none cares whether it prevail or not.

The Rainbow

A stately rainbow came and stood,
  When I was young, in High-Hurst Park;
Its bright feet lit the hill and wood
  Beyond, and cloud and sward were dark;
And I, who thought the splendour ours
  Because the place was, towards it flew,
And there, amidst the glittering showers,
  Gazed vainly for the glorious view.
With whatsoever's lovely, know
  It is not ours; stand off to see,
Or beauty's apparition so
  Puts on invisibility.

The Revelation

An idle poet, here and there,
Looks round him; but, for all the rest,
The world, unfathomably fair,
Is duller than a witling's jest.
Love wakes men, once a lifetime each;
They lift their heavy lids, and look;
And, lo, what one sweet page can teach,
They read with joy, then shut the book.
And some give thanks, and some blaspheme
And most forget; but, either way,
That and the Child's unheeded dream
Is all the light of all their day.

CHARLES BAGOT CAYLEY

The Cool of the Morning

Low, as I loved in childhood well,
   The lips of waves, that fling
On tawny sand the pearly shell,
      Are murmuring

From bay so marbled, that one light
   Curl on it hardly shows;
Its boundaries with the sphere unite
      In mist that glows.

The gathering ardours of the Noon,
   The storms that Eve may scare,
The solemn pageant of the Moon,
  Are folded there.

Here children play, and counterfeit
   The golden shows of life—
Nor guess how parching's Passion's heat,
How wild is strife!

How long and weariful their Day
   To mortals may be given!
How sweet and grand and far away
      Are the eyes of Heaven!

Rhyming Games

Byron: My wife's a vixen spoilt by her Mamma
Lady Byron: Oh how I pity poor hen-pecked Papa.

Lady Byron: The lord defend us from a honeymoon
Byron: Our cares commence our comforts end so soon.

Byron: This morn's the first of many a happy year—
Lady Byron: I could not live so long with you, my dear

Byron: O ever in my heart the last and first—
Lady Byron: And without doubt—it is the very worst.

Lady Byron: Perplexed in the extreme to find a line
Byron: A different destiny is yours and mine.

Byron: If rhymes be omens what a fate is ours—
Lady Byron: And bread and butter eagerly devours.

Lady Byron: My husband is the greatest goose alive
Byron: I feel that I have been a fool to wive.

Lady Byron: This weather makes our noses blue
Byron: Bell—that but rhymes an epithet for you.

LORD BYRON

from Fare Thee Well

Fare thee well! and if for ever,
Still for ever, fare thee well:
Even though unforgiving, never
Against thee shall my heart rebel.

Would that breast were bared before thee
Where thy head so oft hath lain,
While that placid sleep came over thee
Which thou never canst know again:

Would that breast, by thee glanced over,
Every inmost thought could show!
Then thou wouldst at last discover
It was not well to spurn it so.

Though the world for this commend thee—
Though it smile upon the blow,
Even its praise must offend thee,
Founded on another's woe:

Though my many faults defaced me,
Could no other arm be found,
Than the one which once embraced me,
To inflict a cureless wound?

Yet, oh yet, thyself deceive not;
Love may sink by slow decay,
But by sudden wrench, believe not
Hearts can thus be torn away:

Still thine own its life retaineth,
Still must mine, though bleeding, beat;
And the undying thought which paineth
Is—that we no more may meet.

GEORGE MACDONALD

To Lady Noel Byron

Men sought, ambition's thirst to slake,
The lost elixir old
Whose magic touch should instant make
The meaner metals gold.

A nobler alchymy is thine
Which love from pain doth press:
Gold in thy hand becomes divine,
Grows truth and tenderness.

Gone from Wars

A tattered soldier, gone the glow and gloss,
With wounds half healed, and sorely trembling knee,
Homeward I come, to claim no victory-cross:
I only faced the foe, and did not flee.

The Homeless Ghost

Still flowed the music, flowed the wine.
  The youth in silence went;
Through naked streets, in cold moonshine,
  His homeward way he bent,
Where, on the city's seaward line,
  His lattice seaward leant.

He knew not why he left the throng,
  But that he could not rest;
That something pained him in the song,
  And mocked him in the jest;
And a cold moon-glitter lay along
  One lovely lady's breast.

He sat him down with solemn book
  His sadness to beguile;
A skull from off its bracket-nook
  Threw him a lipless smile;
But its awful, laughter-mocking look,
  Was a passing moonbeam's wile.

An hour he sat, and read in vain,
  Nought but mirrors were his eyes;
For to and fro through his helpless brain,
  Went the dance's mysteries;
Till a gust of wind against the pane,
  Mixed with a sea-bird's cries,
And the sudden spatter of drifting rain

Bade him mark the altered skies.
The moon was gone, entombed in cloud;
  The wind began to rave;
The ocean heaved within its shroud,
  For the dark had built its grave;
But like ghosts brake forth, and cried aloud,
  The white crests of the wave.

Big rain. The wind howled out, aware
 Of the tread of the watery west;
The windows shivered, back waved his hair,
 The fireside seemed the best;
But lo! a lady sat in his chair,
 With the moonlight across her breast.

The moonbeam passed. The lady sat on.
 Her beauty was sad and white.
All but her hair with whiteness shone,
 And her hair was black as night;
And her eyes, where darkness was never gone,
 Although they were full of light.

But her hair was wet, and wept like weeds
 On her pearly shoulders bare;
And the clear pale drops ran down like beads,
 Down her arms, to her fingers fair;
And her limbs shine through, like thin-filmed seeds,
 Her dank white robe's despair.

She moved not, but looked in his wondering face,
 Till his blushes began to rise;
But she gazed, like one on the veiling lace,
 To something within his eyes;
A gaze that had not to do with place,
 But thought and spirit tries.

Then the voice came forth, all sweet and clear,
 Though jarred by inward pain;
She spoke like one that speaks in fear
 Of the judgment she will gain,
When the soul is full as a mountain-mere,
 And the speech, but a flowing vein.

"Thine eyes are like mine, and thou art bold;
 Nay, heap not the dying fire;
It warms not me, I am too cold,
 Cold as the churchyard spire;
If thou cover me up with fold on fold,
 Thou kill'st not the coldness dire."

Her voice and her beauty, like molten gold,
 Thrilled through him in burning rain.
He was on fire, and she was cold,
 Cold as the waveless main;
But his heart-well filled with woe, till it rolled
 A torrent that calmed him again.

"Save me, Oh, save me!" she cried; and flung
 Her splendour before his feet—
"I am weary of wandering storms among,
 And I hate the mouldy sheet;
I can dare the dark, wind-vexed and wrung,
 Not the dark where the dead things meet."

"Ah! though a ghost, I'm a lady still—"
 The youth recoiled aghast.
With a passion of sorrow her great eyes fill;
 Not a word her white lips passed.
He caught her hand; 'twas a cold to kill,
 But he held it warm and fast.

"What can I do to save thee, dear?"
 At the word she sprang upright.
To her ice-lips she drew his burning ear,
 And whispered—he shivered—she whispered light.
She withdrew; she gazed with an asking fear;
 He stood with a face ghost-white.

"I wait—ah, would I might wait!" she said;
 "But the moon sinks in the tide;
Thou seest it not; I see it fade,
 Like one that may not bide.
Alas! I go out in the moonless shade;
 Ah, kind! let me stay and hide."

He shivered, he shook, he felt like clay;
 And the fear went through his blood;
His face was an awful ashy grey,
 And his veins were channels of mud.
The lady stood in a white dismay,
 Like a half-blown frozen bud.

"Ah, speak! am I so frightful then?
 I live; though they call it death;
I am only cold—say dear again"—
 But scarce could he heave a breath;
The air felt dank, like a frozen fen,
 And he a half-conscious wraith.

"Ah, save me!" once more, with a hopeless cry,
 That entered his heart, and lay;
But sunshine and warmth and rosiness vie
 With coldness and moonlight and grey.
He spoke not. She moved not; yet to his eye,
 She stood three paces away.

She spoke no more. Grief on her face
 Beauty had almost slain.
With a feverous vision's unseen pace
 She had flitted away again;
And stood, with a last dumb prayer for grace,
 By the window that clanged with rain.

He stood; he stared. She had vanished quite.
 The loud wind sank to a sigh;
Grey faces without paled the face of night,
 As they swept the window by;
And each, as it passed, pressed a cheek of fright
 To the glass, with a staring eye.

And over, afar from over the deep,
 Came a long and cadenced wail;
It rose, and it sank, and it rose on the steep
 Of the billows that build the gale.
It ceased; but on in his bosom creep
 Low echoes that tell the tale.

He opened his lattice, and saw afar,
 Over the western sea,
Across the spears of a sparkling star,
 A moony vapour flee;
And he thought, with a pang that he could not bar,
 The lady it might be.

He turned and looked into the room;
 And lo! it was cheerless and bare;
Empty and drear as a hopeless tomb—
 And the lady was not there;
Yet the fire and the lamp drove out the gloom,
 As he had driven the fair.

And up in the manhood of his breast,
 Sprang a storm of passion and shame;
It tore the pride of his fancied best
 In a thousand shreds of blame;
It threw to the ground his ancient crest,
 And puffed at his ancient name.

He had turned a lady, and lightly clad,
  Out in the stormy cold.
Was she a ghost?—Divinely sad
  Are the guests of Hades old.
A wandering ghost? Oh! terror bad,
  That refused an earthly fold!

And sorrow for her his shame's regret
  Into humility wept;
He knelt and he kissed the footprints wet,
  And the track by her thin robe swept;
He sat in her chair, all ice-cold yet,
  And moaned until he slept.

He woke at dawn. The flaming sun
  Laughed at the bye-gone dark.
"I am glad," he said, "that the night is done,
  And the dream slain by the lark."
And the eye was all, until the gun
  That boomed at the sun-set—hark!

And then, with a sudden invading blast,
  He knew that it was no dream.
And all the night belief held fast,
  Till thinned by the morning beam.
Thus radiant mornings and pale nights passed
  On the backward-flowing stream.

He loved a lady with heaving breath,
  Red lips, and a smile always;
And her sighs an odour inhabiteth,
  All of the rose-hued may;
But the warm bright lady was false as death,
  And the ghost is true as day.

And the spirit-face, with its woe divine,
 Came back in the hour of sighs;
As to men who have lost their aim, and pine,
 Old faces of childhood rise:
He wept for her pleading voice, and the shine
 Of her solitary eyes.

And now he believed in the ghost all night,
 And believed in the day as well;
And he vowed, with a sorrowing tearful might,
 All she asked, whatever befell,
If she came to his room, in her garment white,
 Once more at the midnight knell.

She came not. He sought her in churchyards old
 That lay along the sea;
And in many a church, when the midnight tolled,
 And the moon shone wondrously;
And down to the crypts he crept, grown bold;
 But he waited in vain: ah me!

And he pined and sighed for love so sore,
 That he looked as he were lost;
And he prayed her pardon more and more,
 As one who had sinned the most;
Till, fading at length, away he wore,
 And he was himself a ghost.

But if he found the lady then,
 The lady sadly lost,
Or she had found amongst living men
 A love that was a host,
I know not, till I drop my pen,
 And am myself a ghost.

The Shortest and Sweetest of Songs

Come
Home.

BESSIE RAYNER PARKES

Hastings In April

In this rejoicing time, when sun and shower
In shining alternation rule the sky,
And the brown fields are shadowed every hour
By cloudy masses scudding swiftly by;
Fields soon to smile in greenness, when the breeze
Leaves on the placid water tracks of light,
Or, hurrying, dimples all the crystal seas
With flecking foam and little wavelets bright—

Then every flower sings out its joyous song;
The wood-anemones, and violets after,
Springing in every Sussex hedge and shaw,
Make all beholders glad with April laughter.
The primrose opens all her folded buds
In yellow beauty to the wooing sun;
Beneath, through banks her lavish bounty studs,
The fretting streams over stones and branches run.

The celandine, and lilac lady's smock,
Warning the gatherer of the cuckoo near;
The white oxalis, and each old grey rock,
Whence glossy ferns hang down, to artists dear,
In every graceful group; the knotted stumps
Embroidered with green ivy, the bare down,
With wind-clipped oaks securely set in clumps,
Meet our glad eyes, emerging from the town.

At every step we take the cattle stare
With great soft eyes, which ask when summer's coming,
And days of grateful heat and tranquil air,
Wherein their lazy worships bask till gloaming.
Fast run the little dogs, and snuff the earth,
Or chase the flying birds with vain endeavour;
The cat considers if to venture forth
And greet on sunny flags the warmer weather.

Round go the windmill-sails, and children swarm
At various games; the sick come slowly walking,
Released by this spring day, and you and I
Will pace the High Street for an hour's grave talking—
I mean that raised and sunny pavement, high
Above the road, and bounded by a wall
Which dear green trees overhang, quite undisturbed,
Save where our meditative shadows fall—

Or out into the country, to that bank
Of blue-bell and red orchis, you with drawing,
And I with Tennyson; no creature near
But the quiet donkey peacefully hee-hawing
Over the hedge. So much for Hastings' treasures
Of sight or sound in April. Every time
Of the long year hath others, beautiful,
Gladdening the heart, and meet for duteous rhyme.

EDMUND WALLER

Old Age

The seas are quiet when the winds give over;
So calm are we when passions are no more.
For then we know how vain it was to boast
Of fleeting things, so certain to be lost.
Clouds of affection from our younger eyes
Conceal that emptiness which age descries.

The soul's dark cottage, battered and decayed,
Lets in new light through chinks that Time hath made:
Stronger by weakness, wiser men become
As they draw near to their eternal home.
Leaving the old, both worlds at once they view
That stand upon the threshold of the new.

Hastings

Old Hastings town, you've given us happy days,
'Neath August sun and grey December cloud.
Excursion trains have not yet disendowed
Your streets of charm. Bank holiday's worst phase
Tries its bad best. But your old fashioned ways
Tempt not its votaries from the beach-bound crowd.
You're still yourself: and it must be allowed
That nowadays that's no mean sort of praise,
                    Old Hastings Town.

The black wood houses, clustered 'neath the cliff,
We watch with fond and jealous eyes each year,
Lest iron-brained Improvement, drawing near,
Should pluck them down. For if it did—ah, if!—
Why, then, for us Farewell, O! pleasant, dear,
                    Old Hastings Town.

LEWIS CARROLL

A Sea Dirge

There are certain things—a spider, a ghost,
The income-tax, gout, an umbrella for three—
That I hate, but the thing that I hate the most
Is a thing they call the SEA.

Pour some salt water over the floor—
Ugly I'm sure you'll allow it to be:
Suppose it extended a mile or more,
That's very like the SEA.

Beat a dog till it howls outright—
Cruel, but all very well for a spree;
Suppose that one did so day and night,
That would be like the SEA.

I had a vision of nursery-maids;
Tens of thousands passed by me—
All leading children with wooden spades,
And this was by the SEA.

Who invented those spades of wood?
Who was it cut them out of the tree?
None, I think, but an idiot could—
Or one that loved the SEA.

It is pleasant and dreamy, no doubt, to float
With 'thoughts as boundless, and souls as free';
But suppose you are very unwell in a boat,
How do you like the SEA?

There is an insect that people avoid
(Whence is derived the verb 'to flee')
Where have you been by it most annoyed?
In lodgings by the SEA.

If you like coffee with sand for dregs,
A decided hint of salt in your tea,
And a fishy taste in the very eggs—
By all means choose the SEA.

And if, with these dainties to drink and eat,
You prefer not a vestige of grass or tree,
And a chronic state of wet in your feet,
Then—I recommend the SEA.

For I have friends who dwell by the coast,
Pleasant friends they are to me!
It is when I'm with them I wonder most
That anyone likes the SEA.

They take me a walk: though tired and stiff,
To climb the heights I madly agree:
And, after a tumble or so from the cliff,
They kindly suggest the SEA.

I try the rocks, and I think it cool
That they laugh with such an excess of glee,
As I heavily slip into every pool,
That skirts the cold, cold SEA.

from Melancholetta

With saddest music all day long
  She soothed her secret sorrow:
At night she sighed "I fear 'twas wrong
  Such cheerful words to borrow.
Dearest, a sweeter, sadder song
  I'll sing to thee tomorrow."

I thanked her, but I could not say
  That I was glad to hear it:
I left the house at break of day,
  And did not venture near it
Till time, I hoped, had worn away
  Her grief, for nought could cheer it!

My dismal sister! Couldst thou know
  The wretched home thou keepest!
Thy brother, drowned in daily woe,
  Is thankful when thou sleepest;
For if I laugh, however low,
  When thou art awake, thou weepest!

Jabberwocky

'Twas brillig, and the slithy toves
    Did gyre and gimble in the wabe:
All mimsy were the borogoves,
    And the mome raths outgrabe.

"Beware the Jabberwock, my son!
    The jaws that bite, the claws that catch!
Beware the Jubjub bird, and shun
    The frumious Bandersnatch!"

He took his vorpal sword in hand;
    Long time the manxome foe he sought—
So rested he by the Tumtum tree
    And stood awhile in thought.

And, as in uffish thought he stood,
    The Jabberwock, with eyes of flame,
Came whiffling through the tulgey wood,
    And burbled as it came!

One, two! One, two! And through and through
    The vorpal blade went snicker-snack!
He left it dead, and with its head
    He went galumphing back.

"And hast thou slain the Jabberwock?
    Come to my arms, my beamish boy!
O frabjous day! Callooh! Callay!"
    He chortled in his joy.

'Twas brillig, and the slithy toves
    Did gyre and gimble in the wabe:
All mimsy were the borogoves,
    And the mome raths outgrabe.

EDWARD LEAR

Four Local Limericks

There was an old person of Rye,
Who went up to town on a fly;
But they said, "If you cough, you are safe to fall off!
You abstemious old person of Rye!"

*

There was an old Lady of Winchelsea,
Who said, "If you needle or pin shall see
On the floor of my room, sweep it up with the broom!"
The exhaustive old Lady of Winchelsea!

*

The was an old person of Pett,
Who was partly consumed by regret;
He sate in a cart, and ate cold apple tart,
Which relieved that old person of Pett.

*

There was an Old Man of the Coast,
Who placidly sat on a post;
But when it was cold he relinquished his hold,
And called for some hot buttered toast.

The Owl and the Pussy-Cat

I

The Owl and the Pussy-cat went to sea
  In a beautiful pea-green boat,
They took some honey, and plenty of money,
  Wrapped up in a five-pound note.
The Owl looked up to the stars above,
  And sang to a small guitar,
"O lovely Pussy! O Pussy, my love,
What a beautiful Pussy you are,
      You are,
      You are!
What a beautiful Pussy you are!"

II

Pussy said to the Owl, "You elegant fowl!
  How charmingly sweet you sing!
O let us be married! too long we have tarried:
  But what shall we do for a ring?"
They sailed away, for a year and a day,
  To the land where the Bong-Tree grows
And there in a wood a Piggy-wig stood
  With a ring at the end of his nose,
      His nose,
      His nose,
  With a ring at the end of his nose.

III

"Dear Pig, are you willing to sell for one shilling
  Your ring?" Said the Piggy, "I will."
So they took it away, and were married next day
  By the Turkey who lives on the hill.
They dined on mince, and slices of quince,
  Which they ate with a runcible spoon;
And hand in hand, on the edge of the sand,
  They danced by the light of the moon,
      The moon,
      The moon,
They danced by the light of the moon.

How Pleasant it is to know Mr Lear

"How pleasant to know Mr Lear!

Who has written such volumes of stuff!
Some think him ill-tempered and queer,

But a few think him pleasant enough.
His mind is concrete and fastidious,

His nose is remarkably big;
His visage is more or less hideous,

His beard it resembles a wig.
He has ears, and two eyes, and ten fingers,

Leastways if you reckon two thumbs;
Long ago he was one of the singers,

But now he is one of the dumbs.
He sits in a beautiful parlour,

With hundreds of books on the wall;
He drinks a great deal of Masala,

But never gets tipsy at all.
He has many friends, lay men and clerical,

Old Foss is the name of his cat;
His body is perfectly spherical,

He weareth a runcible hat.
When he walks in waterproof white,

The children run after him so!
Calling-out, "He's come out in his night—

Gown! That crazy old Englishman! Oh!"
He weeps by the side of the ocean,

He weeps on the top of the hill;
He purchases pancakes and lotion,

And chocolate shrimps from the mill.
He reads, but he cannot speak, Spanish,

He cannot abide ginger beer:
Ere the days of his pilgrimage vanish,

How pleasant to know Mr Lear!

MARRIOTT EDGAR

The Battle of Hastings

I'll tell of the Battle of Hastings,
As happened in days long gone by,
When Duke William became King of England,
And 'Arold got shot in the eye.

It were this way—one day in October
The Duke, who were always a toff
Having no battles on at the moment,
Had given his lads a day off.

They'd all taken boats to go fishing,
When some chap in t' Conqueror's ear
Said 'Let's go and put breeze up the Saxons;'
Said Bill—'By gum, that's an idea.'

Then turning around to his soldiers,
He lifted his big Norman voice,
Shouting—'Hands up who's coming to England.'
That was swank 'cos they hadn't no choice.

They started away about tea-time—
The sea was so calm and so still,
And at quarter to ten the next morning
They arrived at a place called Bexhill.

King 'Arold came up as they landed—
His face full of venom and 'ate—
He said 'If you've come for Regatta
You've got here just six weeks too late.'

At this William rose, cool but 'aughty,
And said 'Give us none of your cheek;
You'd best have your throne re-upholstered,
I'll be wanting to use it next week.'

When 'Arold heard this 'ere defiance,
With rage he turned purple and blue,
And shouted some rude words in Saxon,
To which William answered— 'And you.'

'Twere a beautiful day for a battle;
The Normans set off with a will,
And when both sides was duly assembled,
They tossed for the top of the hill.

King 'Arold he won the advantage,
On the hill-top he took up his stand,
With his knaves and his cads all around him,
On his 'orse with his 'awk in his 'and.

The Normans had nowt in their favour,
Their chance of a victory seemed small,
For the slope of the field were against them,
And the wind in their faces an' all.

The kick-off were sharp at two-thirty,
And soon as the whistle had went
Both sides started banging each other
'Til the swineherds could hear them in Kent.

The Saxons had best line of forwards,
Well armed both with buckler and sword—
But the Normans had best combination,
And when half-time came neither had scored.

So the Duke called his cohorts together
And said—'Let's pretend that we're beat,
Once we get Saxons down on the level
We'll cut off their means of retreat.'

So they ran—and the Saxons ran after,
Just exactly as William had planned,
Leaving 'Arold alone on the hill-top
On his 'orse with his 'awk in his 'and.

When the Conqueror saw what had happened,
A bow and an arrow he drew;
He went right up to 'Arold and shot him.
He were off-side, but what could they do?

The Normans turned round in a fury,
And gave back both parry and thrust,
Till the fight were all over bar shouting,
And you couldn't see Saxons for dust.

And after the battle were over
They found 'Arold so stately and grand,
Sitting there with an eye-full of arrow
On his 'orse with his 'awk in his 'and.

NOTES ON THE MODERN POETS

SALENA GODDEN FRSL is an award-winning novelist, poet and broadcaster of Jamaican-Irish mixed heritage. Her debut novel *Mrs Death Misses Death* won the Indie Book Awards for Fiction and the People's Book Prize, and was shortlisted for the British Book Awards and the Gordon Burn Prize. Her new full poetry collection *With Love, Grief and Fury* and literary childhood memoir *Springfield Road—A Poets Childhood Revisited* were published with Canongate with a double book launch in May 2024. Her work has been widely published, anthologised and broadcast on BBC radio, TV and film.

One of Britain's foremost contemporary poets, Salena's electrifying live performances have earned her a devoted following. A second novel set in the *Mrs Death Misses Death* universe is due for publication with Canongate in 2026. Rough Trade Books published a hardback edition of *Pessimism is for Lightweights—30 pieces of Courage and Resistance* in 2023. The title poem is on permanent display at The People's History Museum, Manchester.

Her poem 'While Justice Waits' was highly commended and published by The Forward Prize 2024. She is a Fellow of the Royal Society of Literature, an Honorary Fellow of West Dean, Sussex and a Patron of Hastings Book Festival and Patron of LIVEwire Poetry — a new UK poetry organisation specialising in writer development and live events. A consistent supporter of the work of other poets, writers and artists, Salena Godden co-hosts a monthly arts and culture radio show and podcast Roaring 20's Radio for Soho Radio with her friends, art journalist Amah-Rose Abrams and poet Matt Abbott.

RICHARD NEWHAM-SULLIVAN was born and raised in St Leonards. He grew up attending local poetry nights and events with his mum, Theresa Sullivan. In his early teens, he started performing at events too. He went on to study Creative Writing at UEA, attaining a First Class Degree, and later gained a Master's from Goldsmiths. After returning to Hastings following his studies, he taught creative writing and poetry around local schools and became a committee member for the Word About Town Festival, as well as running events himself.

He has written three collections of poetry: *The Zoo Keeper* (2003) with photographs by Camilla Stapleton-Hibbert, *Orbiting* (2009) with illustrations by Ed Boxall, and *Things You Don't Know About You* (2020). His first book, *The Zoo Keeper*, was highly commended by the Forward Prize and was the first ever book published by Egg Box Press. *Things You Don't Know About You* includes international McLellan prize-winning poems, 'Two Truths' and 'Paperchains'.

Richard created the *Poet Town* project to bring writers together and celebrate the poets of Hastings.

(In order of first names)

ALEXANDRA (AK) BENEDICT is an internationally bestselling author of crime and mystery novels. Her recent books include *Little Red Death* and *The Christmas Jigsaw Murders*, published by Simon & Schuster. She is also known for her award-winning scripts and high-concept speculative novels. Alexandra has been longlisted for the Golden Dagger and won a Scribe Award for her *Doctor Who* adaptations. Her career began in Hastings, where she lived for many years, and she remains closely connected to the area today, living in nearby Eastbourne.

ALICE DENNY is a poet known for her vivid imagery, powerful performances and commitment to raising awareness of LGBT+ issues. She has been a featured poet in *Scene* magazine and her pamphlet *No Fear, No Shame*, published by City Books, was praised by London Grip Poetry Review, which called her, "a charismatic performer of work of devastating candour." Alice has performed at notable events such as Polari and various Pride festivals.

ANNA SOMERSET's first poetry collection, *From the Doggerlanders*, was published in May 2024 by London Poetry Books. Her work has been featured in the Morecambe Poetry Festival's anthology, the *Lampeter Review*, and her poem about her father's dementia was shortlisted for the Alzheimer's Society Poem of the Year. Anna's poems have been broadcast on East London Radio and were included in the US filmed anthology series *Outdoor Verses in an Indoor World*.

ANNE ROUSE has been featured in *Poetry Review*, *The Guardian*, and *The Times Literary Supplement*, while her books, published by Bloodaxe, have earned critical praise and twice received Poetry Book Society Recommendations. *The Upshot: New and Selected Poems* (2008) was named a TLS Book of the Year. Her most recent collection is *Ox-Eye* (2022). A long-term resident of St. Leonards, she has read at many local events and has collaborated with local artists on projects and performances, including with Emily Johns on the exhibition *Conscious Oil*.

ANNY KNIGHT moved to St Leonards seven years ago and has been working on a sequence of poems about living in the area and its past. At 75 years old, she has a long history of performance poetry. She has performed at Hastings Pride, Polari, the Manchester Women in Comedy Festival and Maureen Younger's MYComedy events. She has also appeared at the LFEST lesbian festival and the Sappho Women's Festival in Lesbos. Her poems are featured in numerous anthologies.

ARIANA TIKAO is a New Zealand musician, composer and writer. She was awarded an Arts Laureate by the Arts Foundation of New Zealand in 2020 and served as an Ursula Bethell writer in residence at the University of Canterbury (NZ) in 2023. During a month-long stay in Hastings in 2024, she was inspired by local history and landscapes to write her poem 'Trail of Tyrants'. Ariana's debut poetry collection *Pepeha Portal* is due to be published by Otago University Press in 2026.

ARMAND GARNET RUFFO is a major contributor to Indigenous literature and scholarship in Canada and a recipient of an Honorary Life Membership Award from The League of Canadian Poets. He is the author of several celebrated works published by Wolak & Wynn, including *Grey Owl: The Mystery of Archie Belaney* (2021), which examines the life of the famous conservationist born and raised in Hastings. Armand's research into Grey Owl involved travelling to Hastings in the early 1990s, where he walked in Belaney's footsteps and met with the then active Grey Owl Society. His most recent publication is *The Dialogues: The Song of Francis Pegahmagabow* (2024).

BEN BRUGES works in education, is Features Editor for Hastings Independent Press and has poems published in magazines such as *Interpreter's House*, *Banyan Review* and *Write Under the Moon*. He attained a 'special consideration' for The Wee Sparrow Press' ekphrastic competition, Creaking Kettle & Elizabeth Royal Patton Memorial Poetry Competition anthologies. He is a member of Hastings Stanza Group.

BEN FAIRLIGHT is a story-teller and song-writer, whose poetry often appears in the Hastings Independent Press. He has also organised and run a number of Open Mic events. His writing is influenced by his love of music, his passion for environmental issues, and his love of poets such as Mary Oliver and Seamus Heaney. For Ben, using words to share concern and love for the land and Earth's creatures feels like the most fundamentally important thing.

BRIAN DOCHERTY, known to friends as the 'Beach Bard of St Leonards', describes himself as a Glasgow-Irish post-Beat poet. He has published eight volumes of poetry, including most recently *The View from the Villa Delirium* (Dempsey & Windle, 2021). Brian has lived in Hastings for the past decade and is a regular performer at local events, as well as a member of Shorelink Writers, Words for Wellness and the Hastings Stanza Group.

BRIAN MOSES is a million-selling children's poet and author best known for his captivating poetry that often integrates elements of history and everyday life. With over 200 books published, including *The Very Best of Brian Moses* (Macmillan) and *On Poetry Street* (Scallywag), his work is a staple in primary schools throughout the UK. Brian has a strong connection with Hastings and the surrounding towns, living in the area and frequently performing his poetry and percussion shows at local schools, libraries and festivals.

BRYAN "BADGER" SELLER is a book-dealer and self-confessed hustler who has had 56 jobs, 38 addresses, travelled to 30 countries and had an undisclosed number of wives. His poetry performances blend stand-up, stories and aphorisms, often drawing inspiration from his travels. In his mid-50s, Bryan motorcycled across the US, performing at open mic venues as he went, including at the famous City Lights Bookshop in San Francisco. His travel blog, 'Badger's Bonneville', gained over 200,000 hits and secured him a regular guest spot on Ohio Talk Radio. Bryan has lived in Hastings for over 40 years.

BILL WYATT (1942 – 2015) was a prolific poet, translator of Chinese and Japanese literature, and the first Zen Buddhist monk ordained in Britain. Chris Torrance said of Bill: "He may well prove to be the best adaptor and translator of oriental short poems into English of modern times." Along with his

14 collections, he self-published numerous pamphlets. His book *Uncollected Haikai* was serialised on Patreon as a part of the *Poet Town* project. He lived in Bexhill on and off for many years and was an active part of local poetry events and festivals, notably reading at the *Word About Town* festival alongside the Faber poet Maurice Riordan and Anne Rouse.

CATHERINE SWEENEY, based in St Leonards, began her poetry journey in 2020 after careers in chemistry, jewellery and investment consulting. She is currently doing an MA in Writing Poetry at the Poetry School/University of Newcastle. Her poems have been featured in *Between the Lines 2021* by CityLit, *The Galway Review* and the *Bird in a Wilderness* anthology by the Hastings Stanza Group. She recently completed a writing residency at the Great North Museum.

CHRIS ANTHEMUM's poetry blends the personal and political, the mystical and mundane. Born in Epping in 1968 to Sri-Lankan and Austrian parents, and later adopted and raised in London by a Welsh father and Chinese mother, Chris went on to study extensively, achieving a PhD in Applied Mathematics. Their diverse heritage and deep knowledge of science and maths inform their writing. Their work, including the poems 'Colours' and 'One Day the Sun', was shortlisted in a competition judged by Margaret Atwood. Chris has performed their poetry in Hastings and Brighton, and currently lives near Hastings Castle.

DAVE ARNOLD is an eclectic multimedia artist based in Hastings. As a poet, he is loved for his hilarious, brash in-your-face performance style, as well as for his Happy House booklets that delight in surrealism and silliness à la Edward Lear and Spike Milligan. His creative pursuits extend beyond poetry to music, performance art, acting, film-making and photography. Dave has had numerous exhibitions locally and further afield, and has shared his poetry on the BBC and ITV.

DELLA REYNOLDS (aka the Poet in Pyjamas) is a teacher and writer based in St. Leonards, where she has lived for three years. She began writing at the age of 60, following a sudden divorce, channelling her experiences of heartache and breakup into poetry with a humorous twist. Her recent poetry collections include *Marriage, Divorce and Me* (2017) and *Dish me a dollop of Poetry* (2019). Della regularly performs her poetry at spoken word events.

ED BOXALL is a children's writer, illustrator, performer and musician. His most recent books are *We the Wild Ones* and *Umpkin*. He has illustrated many books included the works of Brian Moses and Richard Newham-Sullivan. His artwork appears regularly in galleries around Hastings and further afield. He also runs inclusive and friendly performance events.

EMMA JOLIFFE emerged from the vibrant spoken word scene in London. In 2016, her first poetry collection, *Citizen of Nowhere*, was published by Burning Eye Books. That same year, she moved to Hastings and her focus shifted from performance to the page. Having run the mixed arts night 'The Whole Shebang' at the Printworks from 2017 to 2020, she now conducts writing workshops and collaborates with musicians and artists, drawing inspiration from Hastings' history, people, politics and landscape.

FIONA PITT-KETHLEY is a poet, novelist, travel writer and journalist with over 20 books of prose and poetry to her name. Her most recent collection is *Ninja Virgin* (Hedgehog Press). She has written for The Times, Telegraph, Independent, Guardian and London Review of Books. Fiona lived in Hastings from 1976 until 2002, forming many friendships within the old town artist community. Since 2002, she has resided in Spain with her husband, chess grandmaster James Plaskett. Her upcoming books include *The Samson Crane*, published by Dreich.

GRACE PILKINGTON has performed on the BBC World Service and Times Radio, and at festivals including Hay, Port Eliot and Curious Arts Festival. She was longlisted for the Notting Hill Editions essay prize and the National Poetry Competition. She describes her first book, *I Have No Idea What I'm Doing: Poems on Pregnancy and Motherhood*, as "a collection of poems which chronicle the minefield that is pregnancy and motherhood." She lives in Hastings with her husband and two children.

HARRY LEBOWSKI is known for his impressive spoken word performances. After years of writing privately, he moved to Hastings and found his passion for performance ignited at local events. His recent victory at the Flight Feathers Slam, organised by Lucas Howard, earned him a headline set. Harry also performs at other spoken word nights, such as A Load of Poets, and has praised the inclusive and supportive poetry community in Hastings.

HENRY NORMAL is a poet, writer and TV & film producer who has been instrumental in the production of some of the most legendary British comedy shows of the last 30 years. These include *The Royle Family* (co-writer, first series), *Mrs Merton* (co-writer), and *Gavin and Stacey* (Executive Producer). Henry performs at literature festivals and theatres around the UK and has written numerous books of poetry, including recent collections, *The Fire Hills* (2023) and *A Moonless Night* (2024), both published by Flapjack Press. These collections include poems inspired by the countryside around Hastings, where he now lives. Henry is a patron of the Hastings Book Festival and an active supporter of the local poetry scene.

IAIN SINCLAIR is one of the key figures in contemporary literature. Perhaps best known for his books exploring psychogeography, Sinclair's influence on British avant-garde poetry is no less remarkable. As editor of the Paladin Poetry Series and the Picador anthology *Conductors of Chaos* (1996), he hailed fresh, explorative poets and shone a light on many who would have otherwise been ignored. Iain has a strong connection with Hastings and St Leonards and has been an advocate for the creative arts in the area. He has drawn inspiration from the town for several books, including the celebrated novel *Dining on Stones* (Penguin, 2004) and poetry collections, *Buried at Sea* (Worple Press, 2006) and *Postcards from the 7th Floor* (Pighog Press, 2010).

JANE MIDWINTER was born in North West London but grew up in Hastings, where she still lives. Her first published poem, 'Cynefin', was written for a pamphlet celebrating *The Lost Harp*, a community play written by Peter Cox MBE, which includes poems connected with the ancient town of Rhayader in mid-Wales. Another, 'Three Silences', was recently published by *Wild Court*, an international poetry journal based at King's College London. Separated by lockdown, in April 2020, she and her daughter co-wrote and self-published *Mother & Daughter*, a collection of 60 poems.

JOHN HENDRICKSE (1935-2014) was a South African-born poet who lived in Hastings for over two decades. He was a mentor and much-loved friend to many in the local literary scene, bringing his jazz-infused poetry performances to Other Words events. His collection *Khoi* (1990) was published by New Beacon Press. It delves into themes of identity, displacement and cultural heritage, and is marked by his experiences in apartheid South Africa. The poems included here are from *African New Voices* (Longman, 1997) and explore John's return to South Africa after settling in the UK, along with his growing concern for the future of his homeland.

JOHN KNOWLES is a poet, actor, producer, playwright and local theatre developer. His recent sell-out show, *America Ground The Musical*, is an allegory concerning today's housing crisis, which has a particular relevance to Hastings. John is renowned for his Shakespeare-inspired plays, including *The Twelfth Night Trilogy* and *Caliban's Codex*. Ever since co-founding the cabaret night Don't Feed the Poets and the Word About Town festival in the early noughties, John has been fostering local talent and bringing world-renowned writers and musicians to perform in the town.

JOHN MURRAY completed an English and Creative Writing degree at the University of Warwick and has an MA from the Royal Academy of Dramatic Art. Since moving to Hastings in 2017, his poems have focused on the essence of local spaces and community. He publishes his work in the monthly newsletter *Celebrate the Mountains*, alongside artist Thom Kofoed.

JUDE COWAN MONTAGUE is an artist, writer, composer, film historian, poet and broadcaster. During her decade-long tenure at Reuters as an archivist she penned numerous poems inspired by international news stories, some of which were featured in her collection *For the Messengers*, published by Donut Press in 2011. Her other publications include *The Groodoyals of Terre Rouge* (Dark Windows Press,

2013) and *The Originals* (Hesterglock Press, 2018). Her work has also appeared in poetry magazines such as *The Rialto* and *Poetry London*. Jude runs a fine art print workshop on Kings Road, St Leonards.

JUDITH SHAW is a poet, painter and printmaker whose work appears in publications such as *The Frogmore Papers*, *Fib Review*, *Orbis* and *Bird in the Wilderness*. Judith won the Hastings Book Festival Sussex Prize for Poetry in 2023 and she was shortlisted for both the 2022 Gingko Prize and the Area of Outstanding Natural Beauty Best Poem of Landscape. Since moving to St Leonards more than 20 years ago, she has been active in the local creative community, as well as working as a psychotherapist and educational specialist. Judith graduated with distinction from the Masters in Writing Poetry programme at the Poetry School/Newcastle University in 2023.

JUSTIN COE is a spoken word artist and children's poet, highly regarded for his dynamic performances. His work includes creating *The Guardian* recommended show *The House That Jackson Built*, which toured nationally, and poetry collections *The Dictionary of Dads & The Magic of Mums* (Otter-Barry Books). Justin lived in St Leonards and Hastings in the 1990s-2000s, where he was a key figure in the local poetry scene, performing regularly and compering the Other Words poetry night. He also co-organized the Word About Town festival, which brought prominent poets like Linton Kwesi Johnson and John Cooper-Clarke to the town.

KATIE TAYLOR's practice encompasses spoken word, performance, devising and facilitation. Katie has crafted installations, interactive adventures and one-to-one experiences for festivals (Wilderness; A Curious Town), theatre companies (Coney; Damn Cheek) and universities (City, University of London; University of Cambridge). Across her work, Katie creates environments that prompt conversations, with or without words, to enable shared reflection. She seeks to create connection, intimacy and a safe space for people to play with big ideas together.

KEN EDWARDS is a distinguished poet, editor, writer and

musician who has lived in Hastings since 2004. Closely associated with The British Poetry Revival, Ken has been a pivotal figure in independent-press publishing since 1973. He established Reality Street, which published over 60 titles of innovative poetry and writing, including works by award-winning poets. Following on from this, he co-founded Grand Iota. Recent works include his fifth novel *Grech* (2025), and a memoir *Wild Metrics* (2019). His *Collected Poems* was published by Shearsman Books in 2020.

LUCAS HOWARD (aka Lucas the Peaceful Poet) is a prominent figure in the UK spoken word scene. He organizes and hosts popular poetry events across Kent and Sussex, emphasizing inclusion and diversity. Lucas's debut book, *Of Few Words* (Whisky and Beards Press, 2019), has been praised for its accessibility and seamless integration of visual design and language. His work has garnered admiration from notable poets like John Hegley and Joelle Taylor. Lucas hosts the monthly Flight Feathers event in Hastings, where experienced poets mentor newcomers, and has been a key figure in the promotion of the Poet Town project.

MARTIN APPLEBY is a poet and the founder of Scumbag Press, established in 2021 in Hastings. His first collection *In Pursuit of Expression* was published by Earth Island Books in 2025. Before setting up Scumbag Press, Martin had been publishing the Paper and Ink Literary Zine, alongside several chapbooks and a serialised novel. Scumbag consolidates his publishing endeavours under one roof, embodying a punk ethos with its D.I.Y LO-FI PUNK ROCK PUBLISHING tagline. The press has published twenty chapbooks to date, prioritising the love of literature over profit. It has also recently introduced *The Scum Rag*, a literary newspaper.

MARTIN HONEYSETT (1943 – 2015) was a renowned British cartoonist and illustrator, celebrated for his dark humour, satirical social commentary and distinctive drawing style. His work appeared in publications such as *Punch*, *Private Eye* and the *Daily Mail*. He also illustrated several children's books, including Ivor Cutler's *Gruts* (1986) and his own collection of children's poetry, *Animal Nonsense Rhymes* (1984). Martin moved to Hastings in 1986 and was a regular performer at local poetry events. In 2016, his partner, Penny Precious, curated a retrospective of his work, 'A Taste of Honeysett', at Hastings Museum.

MERLIN BETTS is, in many ways, not a poet. He began with short stories, with attempts to play a film reel in the mind of readers. The minimalist, or parsimonious, style of Chuck Palahniuk appealed, then Raymond Carver—and always the language of film: how spaces that don't look busy can actually be full to bursting. Then came the monk-like Charles Bukowski, and the crowning glory, Dylan Thomas. But Merlin still can't claim to read or write good.

NAOMI WOOD is a multi-disciplinary artist, performer and writer who lives near Hastings. She is known for her unique one woman spoken word show *Gobbess*—a true story of rage, resilience and an "enchanting quest for freedom" (Btn Rock). Her writing workshops aim to liberate people from self-doubt and support them to perform their work. She has run several of these courses for Hastings Writers Workshops.

NICK WEBB is a writer based in St Leonards, with roots in Ireland and Walsall. His creative journey began as a vocalist of the indie rock band Capital, who signed to Fierce Panda Records and released the acclaimed mini-album *Days & Nights of Love & War*. Nick now focuses on capturing the essence of life in St Leonards and Hastings through his writing. He frequently performs at local poetry open mic nights. He is currently working on a debut poetry collection.

OLI SPLEEN was born and raised in Hastings. A poet, exhibiting artist, novelist and musician: his most recent albums include *Gaslight Illuminations* (2019) and *Still Life* (2022), the latter of which was also released as a poetry booklet. Like his novel *Depravikazi*, *Still Life* reflects on his experiences of almost dying from AIDS when he was 22. Oli has performed poetry alongside the likes of Kae Tempest, John Cooper Clarke and Joelle Taylor, as well as with his close friend Salena Godden. He contributed a poem to *Disarm Hate*, an album created to raise funds and awareness following Florida's Pulse nightclub massacre. An active figure in the creative scenes of Hastings and Brighton, Oli often performs with his band The Smithmanthers.

ORNA ROSS is an Irish poet, best-selling novelist of historical fiction and the founder-director of the global Alliance of Independent Authors (ALLi). With a career spanning over 40 years, she has become her own publisher, selling more books independently than through her previous third-party publishers. Her works have received awards such as the Goethe Grand Prize for Historical Fiction and the Gold Literary Titan Award for poetry. Orna's poetry delves into themes of love, time and the interplay between memory and reality, often inspired by the woods and the sea. She moved to St Leonards in 2021 and says she has never felt more at home.

PAUL A GREEN was drawn to Hastings by the town's unique character and its ferment of creative works-in-progress. His poetry collections include *The Gestaltbunker—Selected Poems* published by Shearsman Books in 2012 and more recently, *Shadow Times* (QBS Books, 2019). His poetry has been featured in numerous anthologies and magazines in the UK, Canada and the US. Paul has also made contributions to broadcasting, fiction and drama, with plays aired on the BBC, CBC and elsewhere.

PENNY PEPPER is a poet and award-winning author known for her provocative and humorous exploration of the disability narrative. She has performed widely, including at The London Book Fair and the Royal Albert Hall. Her memoir, *First in The World Somewhere* (Unbound), was published in 2017 followed by her first collection of poetry, *Come Home Alive* in 2018 (Burning Eye). Penny has been a guest on BBC News, Newsnight and BBC Radio 4 including Woman's Hour and Saturday Live and she is also columnist for Byline Times. Penny lives in St Leonards.

PETE BROWN (1940 – 2023) was an influential poet and lyricist best known for his work with the rock band Cream. He co-wrote some of Cream's greatest hits, such as 'I Feel Free,' 'White Room,' and 'Sunshine of Your Love,' as well as forming his own bands. Before his musical career, he was a prominent figure in the British Beat Poetry movement. Pete later moved to Hastings and was active in the local music scene. The poems here are from his final collection, *Mundane Tuesday & Freudian Saturday* (Ridgeway Press, 2016).

PETE DONOHUE is an Irish-born, London-raised writer who moved to Hastings in 1986. Known for his connection to the Beat, Punk and Outlaw poetry movements, Pete's work boldly reveals the sometimes-ignored truths of the local environment and community. Since 2012, he has hosted poetry events and open mic nights, including the longstanding Sheer Poetry. He has published eight chapbooks, three broadsides and a full poetry collection, *Swallowing Paregoric Babies* (UnCollected Press, 2020). Pete helped establish the Hastings Independent Press and serves as its Literature Editor.

REANNA VALENTINE is an award-winning poet and disabled activist, known for their debut solo pamphlet *Mad Again* (Written Off) and the Saboteur Award-nominated *Fragmented Light*, co-authored with their grandmother Carolyn Reed. Reanna was shortlisted for the Zealous Amplify prize, longlisted for the Disabled Poets Prize and starred in the award-winning documentary *Collections of Queer Poets*. Since moving to Hastings in 2023, they have been actively involved in the local poetry scene, performing at various events and festivals.

RICHARD MAKIN is an avant-garde writer, poet and visual artist. His trilogy of novels *Dwelling* (Reality Street), *Mourning* (Equus) and *Work* (Equus) has been described by poet and critic David Caddy as "an extraordinary and distinct achievement". Richard's innovative work has won praise from writers such as Iain Sinclair, Ken Edwards and Louis Armand. His next novel, *Martian*, will be published by Equus Press, while his collection of one hundred sonnets, *Argot Xeno*, was serialised on Patreon as a part of the *Poet Town* project.

STEVE TASANE is best known for his critically acclaimed children's novel, *Child I*, published by Faber and translated into 11 languages. Steve is also a renowned playwright and slam-winning poet. His children's play about the experience of child refugees, *10 In The Bed*, toured nationally in 2024, and his poetry collection of the same year, *Counteroffensive* (London Poetry Book), was praised by Joelle Taylor as "blistering spoken word from one of the fiercest founders of the scene." He lived in Hastings from 2004 to 2017, where he regularly performed at Don't Feed The Poets nights and was a committee member for the Word About Town festival. His most recent collection, *This Book Roars*, released in March 2025, is his first poetry collection for children.

SUSAN J LELLIOTT has lived in Hastings or thereabouts for over a decade. Her poetry explores themes of societal control, self-empowerment and the joy of nature. Influenced by poets such as Brian Patten, Mary Oliver and Gerard Manley-Hopkins, her work has been published in local anthologies and national magazines and she has performed widely. Susan is also an accomplished visual artist and is recently retired from a career in education and community work.

TARA VALENTINE has a background in performing arts and initially wrote poetry and music for personal amusement. In recent years, she shifted from theatre to performing her own writing, gaining significant support and inspiration from the Hastings community. Her work has been recognised with an award from the Mayor for her 'Hastings Women' poem and a top prize in the Hastings Book Festival slam competition in 2024. Tara now hosts local events involving music, poetry, and comedy, and performs as a singer, poet, and comedian.

THERESA SULLIVAN is a Scottish-born poet who has lived in St. Leonards and Hastings most of her adult life. Her strongly rhythmic poetry explores her connection with Hastings, her Celtic roots and spiritual themes. Theresa's work has been praised for "making the mythological personal and transforming the everyday with moments of transcendence" (Nick Hunt). Over the years, she has performed regularly at local poetry events and festivals, often collaborating with other poets and artists. She has two poetry collections, *This Mask I Wear* (2020) and *From Out of the Mud the Lotus Grows* (2023).

THOMAS BOWIE WALKER BARRON is a Pagan Punk Romantic with a passion for writing, music, walking, and dancing. Influenced by Dylan, Nina Simone, Yeats, James Dean, Sitting Bull, and Bowie, he also admires the art of El Greco and Paula Rego. He has performed at many notable venues such as the Moscow Arts Theatre, Hampstead Theatre and Tristan Bates Theatre. Trained at the Central School of Speech & Drama,

Thomas moved to Hastings in December 2022, captivated by the land, sea, and people. He now works for Project Rewild as a Bard and Outdoor Learning Facilitator and is a regular performer at local poetry events.

TIM BARLOW is a popular local poet, known for his witty poems and strong stage presence. A regular at local poetry events and festivals, he recently toured East Sussex libraries with Henry Normal, and performed the opening poem for the 2024 Hastings Book Festival, winning the slam competition at the festival the same year. His first collection *Poems from the Edge of England* takes a sideways look at society in a way that is sometimes serious, often funny and always entertaining.

TIM RICH is a Hastings-based writer, editor and New York Times-bestselling ghostwriter. Raised in Mayfield, he has a background rooted in the High Weald. His poetry has been featured in *Dark Angels: Three Contemporary Poets* (2023) and *And So We Grow* (2024), published by Paekakariki Press. Tim is a regular guest on poetry podcasts such as *Eat the Storms* and *Night Light*, and his work appears in journals like *Stone Circle Review*, *Oscillations* and *Random Spectacular*. His letterpress poem print Landfall was exhibited at the Bloomsbury Festival. Tim is the co-founder of the writing association 26.

YELLOW AND GREEN is an artist, writer, and spoken word poet living in Hastings. Navigating childhood trauma, motherhood and the world around them, their work is a raw, honest exploration of emotions, infused with light and healing. They have performed their poetry at various venues in Hastings, including The Observer Building, Hastings Contemporary, and The De La Warr Pavilion. Yellow and Green won the Hastings Book Festival poetry slam in 2023, gaining the opportunity to perform at the event 'Salena Godden & Friends' the same year.

A NOTE ON THE TEXT

In each case where modern poets made punctuation choices to reflect particular ideas or values, these have been respected. With the classic poems, some edits have been made to make the text more readable for a modern audience, such as keeping to only one punctuation mark where in the original text there were two, and writing the complete word if it was abbreviated in an unfamiliar manner, so long as it would not particularly affect the tone, meaning or meter of the poem.

—RNS

ACKNOWLEDGEMENTS

We are grateful to have received permission from the authors, and where necessary the publishers, to reproduce the modern poets included. The classic poems reproduced here are all within the public domain.

Photographs ©**Maxine Silver** · Poet Town Logo ©**Lucas Howard** · 'Beautifully Unharnessed Poets' ©**Lauren Estelle Jones**: the poems included in the film ©the individual poets · 'A Song to Hastings', 'Lost in Spaces', 'A Spoken Word Love Poem', 'A Sonnet for Blues and Rain' from *Come Home Alive* (Burning Eye Books, 2018) ©**Penny Pepper**, by permission of the author · Extract from *Springfield Road: A Poet's Childhood Revisited* (Canongate Books, 2024), 'Tell Good People Good Things' from *Love, Grief and Fury* (Canongate Books, 2024) 'Under the Pier' and 'When They Took Her Away' from *Under the Pier* (Nasty Little Press, 2011) 'While Justice Waits' first published in the Forward Book of Poetry 2024 (Faber & Faber, 2024), 'Foreword' of this anthology ©**Salena Godden**, by permission of the author · 'The Gods of Green Summer are Awake', 'To the Gods of Green Summer' & 'No Trains Home' ©**Ed Boxall**, by permission of the author, · 'Dungeness' & 'Dragon Path' from *Lost Magic: The Very Best of Brian Moses* (Macmillan Children's Books, 2016) 'Those 1066, Battle of Hastings, Re-enactment Blues' ©**Brian Moses**, by permission of the author · 'The Selection Process' was first published in Magma, 2016 ©**Alexandra Benedict**, by permission of the author · 'I'm Going Over The Country Park' ©**Reanna Valentine**, by permission of the author · 'The Big Sainsbury's' and 'The Dead' ©**John Murray**, by permission of the author · 'Buffalo Bill's Wild West Show Comes to Hastings', 'Wa-Sha-Quon-Asin', 'He Who Walks By Night', 'Morning After, Toronto 1936', 'Grey Owl, 1937' from *Grey Owl: The Mystery of Archie Belaney* (Coteau Books, 1996 & Wolak & Wynn, 2021) ©**Armand Garnet Ruffo**, by permission of the author · 'Deer' first published in *Oscillations*, 'Osiris is slain and his remains distribute about the Internet', 'Forever impossible', 'On the difficulty of selecting the right frame for a portrait', ©**Tim Rich**, by permission of the author · 'Caroline' ©**Alice Denny**, by permission of the author: 'Caroline' refers to lyrics from "Pretty in Pink." Psychedelic

(Knight Books, 1986) ©**Martin Honeysett**, by permission of the author's family · 'Good Sport' ©**Della Reynolds**, by permission of the author · 'Hastings is' & 'Battle Rap' ©**Steve Tasane**, by permission of the author · 'The Kipper', 'Nature's Highway (a la David Attenborough)' & 'Subj: poem' ©**Bryan Seller**, by permission of the author · 'scattered pins' ©**Jane Midwinter**, by permission of the author · 'Wave Ghazal', 'They Didn't Go Home', 'Like' & 'A Dream of Reclaimed Land' from *Collected Poems: 1975 -2020* (Shearsman Books, 2021) ©**Ken Edwards**, by permission of the author · 'U have to read to write good', 'I, Adrienne' & 'Don't equate me' ©**Merlin Betts**, by permission of the author · 'The Rain' from *The Gestaltbunker* (Shearsman Books, 2012), 'Statement', 'Bedtime' & 'Eleventh Hour'©**Paul A Green**, by permission of the author · 'Greenie' ©**Ben Fairlight**, by permission of the author · 'Trust the Process' ©**Catherine Sweeney**, by permission of the author · 'CONQUEST', 'HELP', 'IMRAN', 'INEVITABLE','THE MOON' & 'seagape, seaanchor, seaash ...' from *Dwelling* (Reality Street, 2011) ©**Richard Makin**, by permission of the author · 'A marriage', 'The Towel' & 'In this poem my mother' ©**Judith Shaw**, by permission of the author · 'Recalling Brigid' ©**Orna Ross**, by permission of the author · 'Nowruz Mubarak?' first published in *The Howling Owl*, 'Abraham's Children' & 'His Ninetieth' first published in *Write Under the Moon* ©**Ben Bruges**, by permission of the author · 'All Gone' ©**John Knowles** · 'Colours', 'Father's Day' & 'One Day the Sun' ©**Chris Whitrow**, by permission of the author · 'Maud' ©**Anny Knight**, by permission of the author · 'Doreen is limbo dancing' & 'Your friend, the Robin, flew in' ©**Anna Somerset**, by permission of the author · 'The Comeback', 'Life in the Necropolis', 'Sometimes the Illusion is Ferocious' & 'Out of Everywhere' from *Things You Don't Know About You* (Moth Light Press, 2020) 'Introduction to Classic Poets' from this anthology ©**Richard Newham-Sullivan**, by permission of the author · 'HAIKU', 'ASHTRAY' & 'STREET BODHISATTVAS, a haibun' from *Even Clouds are Geniuses: Bill Wyatt—his life and work* by Phil Maillard ©**Bill Wyatt**, by permission of the author · 'The Difference Engine', 'Winchelsea Beach in Winter', 'Sit Down Poetry', 'The Fire Hills' & 'Better Days' from *The Fire Hills* (Flapjack Press, 2023) ©**Henry Normal**, by permission of the author

Poet Town: The Poetry of Hastings & Thereabouts is a community-driven, community funded initiative. This project was created to celebrate Hastings and its poets. In addition to this anthology, *Poet Town* has interviews, book serialisations, events and an exhibition. To find out more about the project and get involved, join the Poet Town Facebook group and become a member of Poet Town Patreon.

Thank you to the following people for supporting our very first Crowdfunder:

Bryan "Badger" Seller
Caleb Evans
Chris Whitrow
Della Reynolds
Irina Yelland

Jelka Stgar
Josie Evans
Lee Forster-Kirkham
Sherralyn Fisher
Tim Barlow

This book would never have existed without the generosity, effort, support and dedication of so many people. Many poets included in this book have gone above and beyond to help this project in so many ways. Our gratitude spans from the East Hill to the pier and back again.

www.ingramcontent.com/pod-product-compliance
Ingram Content Group UK Ltd.
Pitfield, Milton Keynes, MK11 3LW, UK
UKHW020229300825

462399UK00001B/4

9 781836 547686